Pathway to Christ

A Christian Workbook

Malachi Mitchell

Copyright © 2019 Anthony Bernard Mitchell
All rights reserved.
ISBN-10: 179427328X
ISBN-13: 978-1794273283

Endorsements

"This book is a **must read** for every Christian. It is filled with fundamental scriptural truths that will challenge you to become who God wants you to be. On the journey to *becoming*, you will have the practical and spiritual tools needed to walk on the right path.

Pathway to Christ is a journey through the Word of God, that will empower you to live your God-given purpose in Christ. It's not just a good read; it's an experience. A powerful, practical and reliable resource that every person of faith need!

This book is not just for reading; but studying and applying. It will increase your biblical knowledge, faith and ability to experience God in a personal and intimate way. You will be empowered to walk the pathway that leads to successful living in this life, while preparing you for the glorious eternal one next."

Jessica Janniere

Speaker

Best-Selling Author, *My Colored World: A Memoir*

"Disoriented about your direction in life? Knowing God's purpose for you will reduce your stress & simplify your decisions, you'll begin living on purpose with PURPOSE!

In Pathway to Christ, Malachi Mitchell answers some of life's toughest and most perplexing questions in simple Scriptural ways that will absolutely revolutionize your spiritual walk! It's time to arise and shine to fully express your gifts and talents, this book will lead you into greater levels of influence and impact as your transformed by its truth!

This is the hour to lead by purpose and passion, as you do, you'll exit mediocrity and come into Extraordinary Living! A groundbreaking book designed to walk you out of confusion into certainty & confidence straight into a life of significance!"

Dr. Roseanna **R**oman
Author | Tv Host | Speaker
Founder of Morning Manna & Kingdom Voice's Ministries

"Pathway to Christ is one of those rare books that come around every once in a while, that is a game changer to those who read and study the principles inside it. This **must-read** book will fill your soul with fundamental scriptural truths that will challenge you to become the person you were created to become.

Very few books will inspire you in a way that Pathway to Christ does, to live your purpose driven life and to live it the way God wants all of us to live it. This book is your GPS to help you live a fulfilled spiritual life."

Greg Walker
Speaker | Coach | Consultant
USA TODAY Best-Selling Author
Dream to Grow Rich: How to Dream ~ Grind ~ Hustle
Your Way to Success

"The Pathway to Christ is an excellent resource tool and definitive guidebook for living a fulfilling and God-driven life. Let's be clear, this is a WORKBOOK, but is more than that, it is an exploration into soul of "man" as we struggle to grow in our walk with God. Malachi provides the reader the practical tools and biblical resources to empower us as we endeavor to lead purpose-driven spiritual life fortified by the word God.

The Pathway to Christ is a definitive resource and study guide for anyone seeking to grow in their understanding and knowledge of Christ's life and message; from those who are "new in Christ" to the experienced Biblical scholar, you will be touched and inspired by Bible-based teachings that Malachi offers. This is a seminal spiritual guidebook to building a spiritual foundation for our spiritual life journey. I highly recommend it!"

Ric Epps
Vice President, Academic Senate
Vice Chair, College Council
Professor
Political Science
Behavioral Science & Social Science Department
Imperial Valley College
richard.epps@imperial.edu

*One way to define spiritual
maturity is when you can study
differing doctrinal viewpoints
enough to understand how people
arrive at their conclusions.
You may not agree with their
conclusions, but at least you have
studied it with enough objectivity
to understand how they arrived at
their conclusions.*

~Richard Wayne Garganta

Acknowledgements

First and foremost, before I start my shout outs, I just want to thank God! I have not always been what one would consider a model Christian all the time. But God kept me. I am so glad that God is a God of a second chances. And in my case... I've lost count how many times.

I have been battling with the thought of writing for many years, even while attending college. Many of my professors suggested that I use the gift that God has blessed me with and write. I never really thought of myself as being a serious writer, but here I am. Lord, I thank you.

Now, on to the shout outs. Lord, please do not allow me to forget anyone! To the love of my life for the rest of my life. My friend, my rib, my encouragement, my everything, and most importantly my wife, Christine, words cannot adequately express how much I love you. Thank you so much for allowing me to be me. If it were not for you, I really don't think I would be writing, or doing many of the exciting things that I am now doing, I really don't think I would even attempt them. You bring the jiggy back in my life. Even though we both know in the beginning you were attracted to me because you thought I was Will Smith's older brother! I love you dearly!

To my parents, Bishop Henry, and Lady Lola Mitchell. I can't thank you enough for being the spiritual examples you have been in my life. It is because of how you raised me I am who I am today. Your love and the countless prayers have not only protected me but guided my entire life.

To my brother Derrick Sr., and his wife (a true-blue sister) Jacqueline. Thank you for being there when I really needed to escape and chill. Thanks for all the tough talks and for knowing that no matter what, life is *"Incredible"*.

To my three wonderful and awesome children, and three fabulous grandchildren. Ashlyn, you are indeed your daddy through and through. I am so proud of you and how you have grown up to be a wonderful mother, and wife to Chuck (a great husband). God is using you to bless the world through your gifts and talents. You have not allowed disappointment and betrayal to hinder God designed purpose in your life. You have risen out of the ashes of traditional dogma to shine bright in darkness and have helped other women and wives to find their way out as well. Y'all don't know? You better ask somebody (www.spicedwife.com). You and Chuck have given me some exceptional grandchildren (Serenity, Saige and Cason; Paw Paw loves you dearly). To my son Anthony "Terrell", you are my pride and joy! And the prince of my kingdom (whatever that is). It makes me incredibly proud to see how you have been molded into the kind of man I knew was trying to be birthed out of that hard and stubborn cocoon. And what emerged was a real man that any woman would be proud and happy to have in her life (especially since you can do her wig). I thank God for you and the gifts that He has blessed you with. Never stop moving upwards! Your past steps in life proves that you are a fighter and a winner. Last, but certainly not least! My Deja "Bug", you are certainly my miracle baby. My shy one! God is crafting your life so wonderfully and you are turning into such a very beautiful young woman. I can hardly wait to see all that you will accomplish. I love you all so very much,

Daddy

To my dearest and most treasured friends, Robert Edwards (and brothers), the late Bishop Antoine Bradford, Rosemary Bradford, Antoine Bradford IV (Way to go BOUY), and Jeremy Bradford, Pastor "JP" and April Prothro, Mimi (Zumba Queen) Wright, Sean Slaughter, Erroll Williams, Kadell Felton, Sr., the Benson's, Willie and Marva Jones, my boy Ernie Thomas (you already know), and to *all* my LGC boy's like my little brotha, "IKE" Walker, all you that I could not list from the Living Gospel Church fellowship; you all have touched my life in a special way. To my GSC (Good Samaritan Church) family (yes you too Fred "Bumpy" Byers); where you lack in number you make up in loyalty and love!

A very special thank you to those that took the time out of their busy schedule to endorse my book, Professor Rick Epps, Jessica Janniere (pronounced Jah-neer), Greg (Big Dreamer) Walker, and Dr. Roseanna Roman. And to my editor, Dani Rene. You are the best! Without you this could not have been accomplished. I am forever in your debt, because that's how long we will be working together!

To the hosts of family and friends thank you for sharing my life.

{If I did not mention you, please know that you are not forgotten. This is dedicated to you!}

Table of Contents

Introduction

For as long as I can remember, learning about the Bible and how to live a life that God would be pleased with, was something I was born into. When I first met both of my parents, they were Christians; God fearing people. In fact, Dad is a Bishop, the senior pastor of the Good Samaritan Church of San Diego. As of the writing of this workbook, he has been in ministry over 50 years, and married to same beautiful woman, for sixty-three blessed years. So hearing about Christ was not something strange in my early childhood because it was a way of life; my pathway. My parents talked it, they walked it, and they taught the Bible in the home and at church.

Growing up I really loved camping, can't figure out for the life of me why because we never went camping! But during six grade camp I got a taste of the outdoors and the love of exploring the unknown. From then on, I just loved being outdoors. As children my brother and I would be sent back to the country where our grandparents lived, in Fairmead, California. for the whole summer. It was where my parents first met as children. I have such great memories of walking through the fields and discovering the many different paths. It was one of the greatest adventures as a child. We just never knew what we might find on one of those pathways. We used to hear so many scary stories while in the country and how, at night, the boogieman would walk those pathways looking for his next victim. It was fun, but nerve-racking.

There are many pathways in life. Pathways that hold the keys to success and failure. There is only one true pathway that will grant you the success in life you desire. Most of our lives we have been told what pathways we should take. These pathways are not of our choosing but are the choice of those doing the dictating. When does it stop? When will it end? It won't! Not until you make the decision to stop listening to people whose pathways are not the pathways you desire to take. The Pathway to Christ shares a simple formula of choosing that right one. You will never be happy until you are living the life you dreamed of; a life filled with people going in the same direction, accomplishing many of the same goals and achieving the kind of success that you long to achieve.

Get ready to read and embark upon a journey that will literally change, not only your life as you read it, but it is guaranteed to change everyone else's life close to you. Often in life people are not aware that the pathway they are traveling, will never get them to their destination. The only way to get to the place you truly want to be... is get off the pathway you are on. Your GPS may be faulty, and you don't even realize it.

This workbook is not filled with empty promises and unreachable goals. This workbook is filled with what it takes to get on that right pathway. No hype. No mumbo jumbo. Just the simple truth. Isn't it about time that someone tells you the truth about how to get on the right pathway and stay on it until you have accomplished your lifelong purpose? Of course, it is! That is why you will buy this book and you will read this book. You will also buy a few for your family and friends. Why be the only one achieving true happiness? You do want others to succeed right? Then "Pay it Forward". You can and you will change. You will declare and decree that you will see changes in the lives of those you love, just by following the simple instructions in this book. There are not too many guarantees in this life, but this I can guarantee. Everyone is on a pathway. It's time to get on the right one... The Pathway to Christ.

The Pathway to Christ is a basic handbook that is a simple step by step informational roadmap to help guide you down the pathway of life, to arrive safely to your new home. Christianity is about walking and living a life of faith. It is not always easy and many of the pathways are scary. And the boogieman (Satan) is certainly looking for his next victim, "Be alert, be on watch! Your enemy, the Devil, roams around like a roaring lion, looking for someone to devour" (1 Peter 5:8 Good News Translation).

Each section will have a lesson on Biblical principles, fundamentals for living a Christian life, and to better understand how to walk in faith. At the end of each of the lessons there will be a short quiz to help reinforce what you have read. This will help you build your knowledge of the Word of God. Learning about God and His pathway for us should be fun enjoyable. It is my endeavor in life to bring back the love of reading and studying the Bible, both individually and as a family. The Bible says, "Study to shew thyself approved unto God, a workman that needeth not to be ashamed, rightly dividing the word of truth" (2 Timothy 2:15 King James Version). As you learn what it is that God has planned, and His purpose for your life, be sure that you stay on the pathway to Christ.

In the Beginning

If you confess with your mouth that Jesus is Lord and believe in your heart that God raised him from the dead, you will be saved. 10 For with the heart one believes and is justified, and with the mouth one confesses and is saved. (Romans 10:9-10 New International Version)

In life and in love, no matter what happens, you can always begin again! You can always start with a new beginning. You may fall time and time again. You may even fail a few times, but know this, you can always get up and start again. The wonderful thing about God is that He is a God of second chances. And if you are like me, not perfect by any stretch of the imagination, He is a God of many chances.

Saul to Paul:

The apostle Paul eloquently wrote to the church in Rome, as he had done so often throughout his life as a follower of Christ (something that he could not always brag about). In his writings, he encapsulating the fundamental basics of the Christian conversion; something that he knew all too well from his own personal conversion on the road to Damascus (Acts 9 New KJV). Paul told those in Rome, "If you confess with your mouth that Jesus is Lord...you will be saved" (Romans 10:9 NKJV). This is an essential act of faith on the part of a new convert (Christian). However, it is important to note that one's audible profession of faith does not save you. Salvation only comes by grace through the gift of our faith, not by the words we speak (Ephesians 2:8-9 NKJV). Therefore, with all Scripture, if we are to truly and properly understand it, the context is of critical importance.

Amazingly enough, at the time that the book of Romans was being written, typically the way a person accepted Christ and confessed Him as Lord, was by way of persecution. In many cases, it resulted in their death. It was a sure thing that if you profess Christ and embraced Him, knowing that persecution was sure to follow, it was the work of the Holy Ghost and an indication of true salvation. Therefore, profession of Christ publicly did not save them. Anyone could shout out loud, "I confess Christ" and not be a Christian, especially from prosecution. However, for those that knew their death was certain, it was because of their confession that they had truly been saved. Only that type of boldness and faith comes in knowing that they belong to Him. They had to have faith in knowing that if they just called out to Him, that they would be saved; maybe not from physical death at that moment but saved in their hearts spiritually. "Whoever calls on the name of the Lord will be saved" (Romans 10:13 NKJV).

Looking at the tenth verse, "for he believes for himself in *his* heart into righteousness and confesses for himself with *his* mouth into salvation." Two key elements here. First, "believe"; it is vital in the Christian's conversion. Second, "confess" or to "confirm", meaning that you are confirming with your mouth outwardly what has taken place (the change) on the inside (the heart) and are thankful for that change. The word "salvation" or "deliverance"; being made free from that which binds you. This was evidence of an individual's genuine salvation. If you are truly saved (set free) you will profess and confess Christ as Lord and Savior. Because faith has already been instilled in their hearts by Christ Jesus, "Now faith is the assurance (title deed, confirmation) of things hoped for (divinely guaranteed), and the evidence of things not seen, the conviction of their reality—faith comprehends as fact what cannot be experienced by the physical senses" (Hebrews 11:1 Amplified Bible).

Saul of Tarsus was the most widely read apostle of all who followed Jesus, due to his own personal conversion. Saul was born to a *Jewish* Family in a city called Tarsus, located in Cilicia around AD 1-5. At a very young age,

Saul received some very prestigious religious training from one of the best Rabbinical schools in Jerusalem. The school was headed up by a well-known Pharisee by the name of Rabban Gamaliel (Rabban meaning teacher). This teacher was highly respected by all in the religious community. Gamaliel was so respected that he stood up to intervene on behalf of Jesus when he was arrested and brought before the Sanhedrin courts (Act 5:34-39 NKJV), it really did not matter how respected he was within the counsel, Jesus was still convicted of a crime He did not commit, which was the sin of blasphemy, and crucified on a cross. It was under Gamaliel's teachings in Tarsus that Saul, later to be known as Paul, developed his proficient familiarity of the Hebrew Scriptures. His educational and professional credentials permitted him to preach in synagogues all over the region.

Tarsus was considered a "free city" of Rome. In the Roman empire there were cities that governed themselves by their own customs and laws. These cities had the privilege of selecting their own magistrates. Being a free city, Tarsus was not subject to having Roman guards stationed at their gates. This fact granted Saul *Roman citizenship*, a privilege that he certainly exercised later on in his life when it was deemed necessary (Acts 22:25-28 NKJV). Why was having a Roman citizenship such a prize to be coveted? Because anyone who possessed such a title enjoyed all advantages of being a Roman citizen, including special treatment (favors and even protection). The wide range of privileges included voting rights in the assemblies, legal institutions, and eligibility to run for civil and, or public offices. It also allowed one immunity from certain legal obligations and taxes. So, as you can see, even in the 1st century, there was partiality and favoritism amongst certain ethnic groups, and it was at the expense of the non-citizens. But truth be told, this dichotomy was something that was written about throughout the Bible and one reason why James wrote about it as being a sin (James 2:1-13 NKJV).

Gamaliel greatly influenced Saul's entire life. Personally, and Spiritually. Saul often traveled from Tarsus to Rome when meeting with other religious leaders. On his way back to Tarsus Saul heard a lot of commotion from a crowd of people yelling and screaming at a man named Stephen. Saul was thirty years of age (not a very young man) that he witnessed the death of Stephen by stoning (Acts 7:58-58 NKJV). This incident took place just a few years after the savage crucifixion of Jesus. It was one of the most shocking displays of Jewish hatred towards Jesus and his followers by the religious authorities that was recorded in the New Testament (Matthew 27:35 NKJV). The stoning of Stephen, a follower of Christ Jesus, was the first recorded introduction of Saul in the New Testament.

Stephen the First Martyr:

Stephen was one of the very first deacons (church officials) appointed by the disciples in the early church. It was a few short years, after the death, burial, and resurrection of Christ Jesus, the new believers began to come together and combine all their resources. In Acts 6:1 English Standard Version it says, "And in those days as the disciples were increasing in *number* there was a complaint of the Hellenist (according to the One New Man Bible, Hellenists were Jewish Israelis who had adopted the Greek ways), against the Hebrews, because their widows were being neglected in the daily service." The Greeks that were there amongst the Hebrew, began to complain about how the service was conducted. And the unfair treatment of some of their members. Even in the early church there were those that complained about things going on in the service of the church. And seeing the disarray in the church, and how the widows were being mistreated, the disciples called the people together and explained to them that their jobs were not to leave the word of God to wait tables and serve food, but to teach and preach (Acts 6:2 ESV).

After sharing the importance of their own jobs and roles as followers of Christ, the disciples chose seven men: Stephen, a man full of faith and *the* Holy Spirit, and Philip, and Prochoro, and Nicanor, and Timon, and Parmenas, and Nicolas, a proselyte from Antioch (Acts 6:5 ESV). These men were of honest report, and full of the Holy Spirit. This was the start of the very first official church deacon board (Acts 6:3), these seven men that were selected to care for or service the church ("service" would be the giving of the food, clothing, and other necessities that were provided by the congregation), and for the widows.

Stephen was very zealous and a true defender of Christ and the gospel (Good News), Christianity was called "The Way" in the first few years after the Holy Spirit came. Stephen's name could imply that he was Greek. He was not a dumb man, as he was well-educated in the history of the Jewish people, a man "full of faith, and the Holy Spirit" (Acts 2:1-4 ESV). He preached *Christ and Him crucified* (cf. 1 Corinthians 1:23 NKJV). His message was about the life, death, burial, and resurrection of Christ. For this he was hated and murdered, by the same mobs that cried out at Jesus' trials, "Crucify him!" (Matthew 26:23-24 ESV). Because Stephen was one that God used in a great way to perform wonders and miracles while in Jerusalem (Acts

6:8-14 ESV), many of the Jews on the outer provinces started to question and argue with him. But because he was full of the Holy Spirit and wisdom (v.9), they could not trip him up. Just as the people tried to trip up Jesus, and as with Jesus (because they could not outsmart the Holy Spirit), they conspired and lied, convinced others to bear false witness against him (v.10). The people lied and accused Stephen of blasphemy of Moses and of God. This was a crime punishable by death according to the Judaism customs and law instituted by Moses in the Old Testament. It was an act of showing contempt; it was to insult and express a lack of reverence toward God. The person who committed the act of blasphemy was put to death by stoning.

Those that accused, or better yet, those bore false witness of Stephen, brought up their false claims to the Sanhedrin (vv.11-12). There were smaller Sanhedrin courts, consisting of 23 lesser judges in each town, but this particular Sanhedrin was known as the great Sanhedrin court (which basically meant "council-chamber". 1901. in Smith Bible Dictionary), or supreme council during the times of ancient Israel. The Sanhedrin council was comprised of 71 of the most religiously educated men in Jerusalem and the high priest, who was recognized as the president of council. Its members were chief priests or vice chief justice, scribes, and elders. Pharisees and Sadducees (the very wealthy Sadducees controlled the house, like our US government today). It is not really known how one was chosen to be a part of the Sanhedrin council.

The charges, (false witnesses), brought up against Stephen claimed that they heard Stephen talking about Jesus, saying that he would destroy the Temple (vv.13-14). This in fact that was not the truth of what Jesus said, nor was he talking about a physical Temple. Going back to the day in question, John 2:13-22 ESV there are accounts of Jesus going to Jerusalem for the Passover of the Jewish people. Jesus wanted to be in the city to be able to present in the Temple. However, when he got there, he noticed the selling of cattle and sheep, doves and those that were exchanging money were seated inside of the house of God! (v.14) This not only broke his heart, but it literally inflamed Jesus to the point that he grabbed a whip and starting whipping many of the merchants in the Temple (v.15). Jesus yelled, "You must take all this from this place, you must not make My Father's House a house of market" (v.16). Now this, in turn, outraged the religious leaders that were following him. These leaders were attempting to find hard evidence on Jesus in order to bring him up on charges.

What gave this man the *right* to whip these people out of the Temple? His disciples then remembered (v.17), that it is written: "The zeal of Your House will consume Me" (Psalms 69:10 NIV; John 2:17).

The Jewish leaders came to him and said, "What sign do You show us, since You do these things?" (v.18). Jesus answered and said to them, "Destroy this temple, (Sanctuary, literally translating one's body: (cf. 1 Corinthians 6:19 NIV; 2 Cor. 6:16) and in three days I shall raise it" (v.19). That was the tipping of the religious scale. How in the world was this simple human being going to destroy a physical structure that took forty-six years to build? (*The temple of Jerusalem that was built by Solomon and was destroyed by Nebuchadnezzar, took the nation of Israel (led by Zerubbabel) some forty-six years to build. This was the second temple, meaning it was still being built on during the time Jesus was on earth. Bible Odyssey*) And he expects to raise *it* in three days? (v.20).

Stephen's defense, detailing and outlining the history of the Jews from the time of Abraham through the prophets, was powerful. Insomuch that when he concluded his message, he stated that it was the Sanhedrin who had killed the prophesied Messiah, Jesus of Nazareth. Those that were there in the crowd got furious and enraged with him, "And all that sat in the council, looking steadfastly on him, saw his face as it had been the face of an angel" (Acts 6:15 ESV). And in Acts chapter 7, "When they heard these things, there were cut to the heart, and they gnashed on him their teeth. But he, being full of the Holy Ghost, looked up steadfastly in to heaven, and saw the glory of God, and Jesus standing on the right hand of God" (vv.54-55). That mob got even more irate and irritated with Stephen and dragged him out of the city; then stoned him (v.58). This is the moment Saul aka Paul comes into our story bringing, us right back to where we left off. The people laid their coats at Saul's feet while they picked up huge rocks to throw at Stephen.

Saul witnessed the murder of Stephen, and while Stephen was being stoned, he called upon God, and said as he kneeled to the ground dying, "Lord, do not hold this sin against them". (v.60). After speaking those words, the Bible says, "he fell asleep" and died.

It was not until the Damascus road experience that Saul, now known as Paul, had the pivotal life changing event (Acts 9:1-22 NKJV). This was the beginning of his new walk in Christ. Saul was on his way to Damascus from Jerusalem after he received official letters from the high priest to round up all those who were now a part of the

Christian faith, back to Jerusalem to be murdered. While traveling on the road to Damascus one afternoon Saul was blinded by an extremely bright light. It was so intense he was knocked from his horse. While on the ground he heard a voice, "Saul, Saul, why are you persecuting Me?" (Acts 9:4 NKJV). Saul answered, "Who are You, Lord?" Then the Lord said, "I am Jesus, whom you are persecuting. It is hard for you to kick against the pricks (thorns)" (v.5) Saul having been struck down blind off his horse, had to be led into the city by his traveling companions he rode with to round up Christians and persecute them, as he is was now unable to see. This was an event that changed Saul's life forever. He went from an assassin for Rome, to an apostle for Christ.

This very event led Saul to his total life altering repentance and his receiving the full baptism of the Holy Spirit while under the care of a prophet named Ananias (Acts 9:17-18 NIV). The last thirty-five years of Paul's life was spent sacrificing, suffering and accomplishing some of the greatest Biblical events known to man. At the blessed age of sixty-six Paul was put to death by beheading with a sword, somewhere near Rome between 62 and 67 AD. But like so many other Biblical events, we shall probably never know the real dates for sure.

An important note to remember here in your new beginning; public confession, baptism, and all works of good deeds, are not the means of salvation, they are the evidence of salvation!

Important events in Paul's life: 2 Corinthians 11:21-33 NKJV

*The witnessing of Stephen's stoning

*Received three years of personal teaching Jesus, while living in Arabia

*Resurrected at least one person from the dead

*Carried out at least five evangelistic journeys

*Visited more than 50 cities

*Five times received thirty-nine stripes

*Beaten three times with rods

*Stoned once

*Shipwrecked three times

*Was Robbed

*Bitten by a snake

*Left out in the cold naked, thirsty and hungry

*Let down a wall in a basket to escape the governor under Aretas the king

*Preached the gospel to Emperor Caesar and his entire household

*Wrote no less than fourteen books (epistles/letters) of the Bible (no other author can say that)

*Trained and instructed other evangelists and preachers of the gospel (John Mark and Timothy)

*Endured more than five years in prison

In the Beginning: Quiz

1. Who was the author of the Book of Romans?

2. This is an essential act of faith on the part of a new convert (Christian):

3. Salvation only comes by _____, through the_____ of our _____, not by the words we _____ (Ephesians 2:8-9):

4. What takes place when someone calls on the name of the Lord?

5. What does Romans 10:9-10 say?

6. In your own words explain what Romans 10:9-10 means to you:

7. Who is the Author of the Book of Acts?

8. What was the name of the city where Saul was born?

9. Where was Saul going when he was knocked from his horse and blinded, and why?

10. Name three events in Paul's life:

    a.

    b.

    c.

Notes to Self:

In the Middle

Count it all joy, my brothers, when you meet trials of various kinds, 3
for you know that the testing of your faith produces steadfastness. 4
And let steadfastness have its full effect,
that you may be perfect and complete, lacking in nothing.
(James 1:2-4 New International Version)

Three essential factors on how to live life during trouble and still have joy: James and Peter.

1. The Joy the World Gives, Is Not the Same Joy That God Gives:

When you accept Christ into your heart, and you begin your new life in Him, it does not mean that all your troubles are going to magically disappear. In fact, at times they may seem to be amplified. If you had bills before you got saved, guess what? You are still going to have those same bills. If you had problems on your job or in your relationship before Christ, well sorry to say, those same issues and problems are going to still be there after receiving Christ. However, (and here's the good news), being that you now have the love of Christ and the Holy Spirit dwelling inside of you, those same issues and problems will be faced with a new attitude. Instead of cursing, fussing, fighting, and running away from the issues, you now turn it over to Christ to help you face them; with His help.

James:

In James' writing to the church, he encouraged, and instruct them to have faith in their trials; that their faith could develop perseverance. The problem that seems to arise with many new believers is that when trouble and tough times come continuously upon them, they begin to question; one their faith, and two, they want to know "why?". How could they experience so much hardship and still have joy? It seems that being in the middle of a crisis is the last place to think of counting anything joyful. Romans 15:13 NIV says, "May the God of hope fill you with all joy and peace as your trust in him, so that you may overflow with hope by the power of the Holy Spirit".

Peter: Five things he was known for

1. Peter was one of Jesus' disciples (Matthew 4:18 NIV); 2. Peter, the one called the "Rock" (Matthew 16:18 NIV). 3. The same Peter that walked on water (Matthew 14:28). 4. He is the same Peter that cut off a man's ear in the Garden of Gethsemane (Matthew 26:51) 5. And the same Peter that denied Christ three times (Matthew 26:69-75). He also dealt with joy in the middle of trials, "In this you rejoice, though now for a little while, if necessary, you

have been grieved by various trials, 7 so that the tested genuineness of your faith—more precious than gold that perishes though it is tested by fire—may be found to result in praise and glory and honor at the revelation of Jesus Christ. 8 Though you have not seen him, you love him. Though you do not now see him, you believe in him and rejoice with joy that is inexpressible and filled with glory, 9 obtaining the outcome of your faith, the salvation of your souls" (1 Peter 1:6-9 NIV).

We see with both James and Peter's passages, they are instructing as to what we should do in the middle of stress, worry, trials, and hardships. James said, "Consider it pure joy…" and Peter says, "In this you greatly rejoice…" Why? Well one good reason is because our trials make us stronger. As stated earlier in James's letter to the church in keeping the faith through trials, "faith develops perseverance". How does this happen? By the testing of our faith, that's how. Peter reassures that, "our faith, which is priceless, will be proved genuine and result in praise to God" (1 Peter 1:7 NIV). Joy is mentioned second of the fruit of the Spirit; it is plentiful and; like a bottomless well of water, there is always an abundance of joy. Even in your darkest nights, when grief from loss seems to overtake you, sadness may overwhelm you, but know that God's joy is there in the middle of it with you.

2. God's Joy Cannot Be Taken Away:

There will come times in your life when all hell is breaking loose and everything around you is in total chaos; it seems like all hope is lost! But it's not. As a believer, you are promised by the Holy Spirit that you will have His constant presence with you. This was a promise even in ancient times, "Be strong and courageous. Do not be afraid or terrified because of them, for the LORD your God goes with you; he will never leave you nor forsake you" (Deuteronomy 31:6 NKJV). We are promised His joy and God says that the joy of the Lord is your strength, "The LORD is my strength and my shield; my heart trusts in him, and he helps me. My heart leaps for joy, and with my song I praise him" (Psalms 28:7 NKJV). This is assured just like our salvation, through the one-time sacrifice of Christ Jesus. John wrote about the joy of the Lord being in us and that it may be complete, "These things have I spoken unto you, that my joy might remain in you, and that your joy might be full (complete)" (John 15:11 KJV).

There are other times in the Bible that talk about the disciples being filled with joy. Acts 13:52 NKJV says, "And the disciples were filled with joy and with the Holy

Spirit". And the jailer that was in charge of Paul and Silas (Act 16:23-24) was filled with much joy, as was his entire house, "And when he had brought them into his house, he set a meal before them; and rejoiced [he was filled with joy], because he had come to believe in God with his whole house" (Acts 16:34).

True joy comes in your walk of faith which can bring with it, trials and tribulations, but also much satisfaction. It takes great faith to be able to live a life that one does not completely understand. "How do you truly trust someone you have never met or seen?". This is a worldwide question that thousands of people have wondered. In order to have this type of faith you must have a true understanding of who God really is and as He is revealed throughout the Bible. Having and knowing about this kind of faith will be discussed later in this course. But be assured, that God's joy cannot be taken away. That's real faith.

3. You Have to Grab onto God's Joy:

Stop whining and complaining! Joy is free, just like salvation. It's a gift and one that is perfect, given by God. Therefore, it is imperative that we reach out and accept God's gift to us. Grab onto it and hold it tight, like it's a lifeline. Your life depends on it! Your happiness relies on it. Your health needs it. Make a conscious, deliberate decision to choose joy every single day over anger, bitterness, and sorrow no matter what.

Take a look at the following examples in the Bible and how believers were faced with severe trails and extreme poverty. Their overflowing joy welled up in generosity that was great in richness, (2 Corinthians 8:2-3 NKJV). In spite of severe suffering, they welcomed, by the Holy Spirit, the message of Christ with joy, (1 Thessalonians 1:6 NKJV). Even when all hope seemed lost, they were encouraged to "Be joyful always" (1 Thessalonians 5:16 NJKV). They lost property but they were still joyful and sympathized with those that were casted into prison because of their faith. It didn't faze them because they knew that they had better and lasting possessions in heaven, (Hebrews 10:34 NKJV). And the best example of them all is in Hebrews 12:2, "Let us fix our eyes on Jesus, the author and perfecter of our faith, who for the joy set before him endured the cross, scorning its shame, and sat down at the right hand of the throne of God".

Throughout the Bible we see the church being persecuted; going through many trials, tribulations and hardships. And just like those that were new in their faith, we must learn how to face our hardships and grab onto God's joy while in the middle of severe persecution or even death. No matter what, choose joy. You will have to face all types of overwhelming odds, sickness, disappointments, heartaches, monthly bills, insurmountable obstacles, many even divorce, bankruptcy and foreclosure. I know it sounds horrific, but you need to know that this is life. However, you will discover that right in the middle of all hell breaking loose, God's joy is true and is there with you. You will find joy in each trial, and you can rejoice greatly with inexpressible joy; full of glory. You will be able to endure whatever comes your way because if you have been saved through faith in Christ Jesus, have all you need. So, grab onto God's joy and hold on tight. "For his anger lasts only a moment, but his favor lasts a lifetime! Weeping may last through the night, but joy comes with the morning" (Psalm 30:5 NLT). Let me encourage you with this, IT'S MORNING TIME! Finding Joy in the Middle of it All... That's Wisdom.

In the Middle: Quiz

1. What are the three essential factors for living life amid trouble and still have joy?

    a.

    b.

    c.

2. When accepting Christ in your heart, does that mean that all problems with cease? Why or why not?

3. Why did James write to the church?

4. Peter was known for:

    a.

    b.

    c.

    d.

5. What does Deuteronomy 31:6 say?

6. True joy comes in your _____ walk.

7. The _____ of the _____ is your _____ (Nehemiah 8:10).

8. No matter what, choose _____.

9. Throughout the Bible we see the church being _____.

10. What should you do with God's joy?

Notes to Self:

What Faith, Now Faith

Now faith is confidence in what we hope for and assurance about what we do not see.
(Hebrews 11:1 NIV)

One of the most important elements in a person's life is faith. You must believe! Whether you are a Christian or non-Christian, faith is the fundamental foundation to everyday life. People all over the world demonstrate faith every minute of the day, knowingly and unknowingly. Hebrews 11:1 NKJV is the true definition of what faith really is. It is trusting in something you explicitly cannot prove. What we believe, is based on what we have heard, what we hear, what was or is said to or around us, and what we are conditioned (programmed) into us by our teachers, parents, siblings and our friends as well as our society when we are children.

There are two aspects of faith: One is Intellectual assent and the other is Trust. The first aspect, Intellectual assent, is the believing of something to be true. Is it true just because you believe it? Does that make it true? Just because I say, "The sky is green, and my grass is blue" does not make it true. The evidence of truth is looking at the sky and grass and *seeing* that it is wrong. The sky is blue, and the grass is green. So, in fact, what I chose to believe to be true was not true at all. How do we deal with that? For years we are told and taught things all our lives. Things that others claim to be true. But as we all grow up and learn what is and what isn't true or correct, we still have a choice to believe it or not. It is called our belief system. We have a choice to continue to believe in it or not. But for someone to continue to believe in something that is not correct is beyond me.

Trust is the second aspect of faith. Trust is relying on facts that something is true. A Chair is the best used example in illustrating these two aspects. In intellectual assent, it is recognizing the chair and coming to an agreement that it is a chair and it was designed to support and hold up a person when they sit on it. Trust, that is literally physically sitting on the chair. Okay, we believe that it is a chair and we believe that it was designed to support and hold a person. But we still must to physically sit in the chair. Similarly, we must fully and personally rely on the death of Jesus as the only atoning sacrifice for our sins, "But God demonstrates his own love for us in this: While we were still sinners, Christ died for us" (Romans 5:8 NIV).

It is crucial to understand these two aspects of faith. When it comes to Jesus, there are many people that believe certain facts about him. Regarding facts about Jesus, many will intellectually agree with the Bible. However, knowing those facts to be true is not what "faith" is meant to be in the Bible. The definition of faith, biblically, requires intellectual assent to the facts and trust in the facts.

Saying you believe in something is a very easy thing to do. However, it is not enough just to believe that Jesus is God incarnated, died on the cross, buried in a grave, and then resurrected on the third day to pay the penalty for our sins. Because the Bible says that even the demons *believe* in God and they also acknowledge those facts, "You believe that there is one God. Good! Even the demons believe that—and shudder!" (James 2:19 ESV). The Bible is clear when it says that faith is the belief one has in the one, true God, without seeing Him.

Where does this type of faith come from? It's certainly not something we dream up all on our own. And it is not something that we are born with. And as much as I enjoy studying and pursuing knowledge, it is not a result of all our diligence in study and the pursuit of spiritual things. Faith is certainly a gift and one that comes from God Himself. A gift that no one can work for. "For by *grace* you have been saved through faith. And this is not your own doing; it is the gift of God, not a result of works, as that no one may boast" (Ephesians 2:8-9 ESV). Simply put, faith is given by God, along with His mercy and grace, according to His perfect will, plan and His purpose for our lives. And He gets all the glory for it.

We must demonstrate our faith and trust in God, because according to the Bible, our faith is very essential to our Christianity. And without faith it is impossible to please Him, (Heb. 11:6 ESV), and without trust in Him, we have no place in Him. Therefore, James encouraged the church in his letter to consider when we fall into trials. It is *pure joy,* because when we are tested in your faith it produces; perseverance, and over time it will mature us; by strengthening our walk. This provides the evidence that our faith is true. "Count it all joy, my brothers, when you meet trials of various kinds, 3 for you know that the testing of your faith produces steadfastness. 4 And let steadfastness have its full effect, that you may be perfect and complete, lacking in nothing" (James 1:2-4 ESV).

The question is, "What increases our faith?". The answer is, *by drawing closer to God through praying and studying His Word.* That seems simple, but in fact there are a lot of people that don't really like to pray and study the word of God. And in order to have a strong relationship with God that is built on faith, we need to be praying (daily) and reading His word (daily). We are inundated daily with worry and stress, not knowing how we are going to make ends meet, when in fact the ends never do meet.

In his letter to the Philippians Paul encouraged them, "Do not be anxious about anything [don't worry or stress] but in every situation, by prayer and petition, with thanksgiving, present your requests to God. 7 And the peace of God, which transcends all understanding, will guard your hearts and your minds in Christ Jesus" (Philippians 4:6-7 ESV).

Three ways how we grow in faith:

1. By confessing our sins (John 1:7 NKJV; 1 John 1:9)
2. By seeking Him (Ps. 27:8 NKJV; Isa. 55:6)
3. By Surrendering to Him (Gal. 3:3 NKJV; Col 2:6; Rom. 12:1)

What Faith, Now Faith: Quiz

1. What is one of the most important elements in a person's life?

2. What are the two aspects of faith?

    a.
    b.

3. What does the Bible say about the demons believing in James 2:19?

4. This is what we believe is based on:

5. What is faith really? (Eph.2:8-9):

6. Without it, it is impossible to please God

_____.

7. James tells us to consider our fall into trials as what?

8. How is our faith increased?

9. In Philippians 4:6-7 Paul encourages the church to

_____.

10. What are the three ways we grow in our faith? (Include scripture ref.)

Notes to Self:

New Creation

*Therefore, if anyone is in Christ, he is a new creation; old things have
passed away;
behold, all things have become new.*
(2 Corinthians 5:17 NKJV)

Everyone loves a new beginning. To be able to start all over again, fresh and new. Whether it's a new job, getting a new car or house, or maybe even starting over in a new relationship. We all like the feeling that comes with something new.

One of the best-known spiritual ways for man to start over is by giving his/her life to Christ. As Paul stated in 2 Corinthians 5:17 NKJV, one of the most quoted scriptures to date, "Therefore, if anyone *is* in Christ, *he is* a new creation; old things have passed away; behold, all things have become new". What is interesting is the word "therefore" which if we would look at the previous verses here, in verses 14-16, Paul writes that all believers have died with Christ and no longer live for ourselves. We are now spiritual and no longer live for the world. Our old sin nature was nailed to the cross with Jesus. It was crucified, it died, and it was buried with Him. And when the Father raised Him up, we too were raised up to *walk in the newness of life,* 'Therefore we were buried with Him through baptism into death, that just as Christ was raised from the dead by the glory of the Father, even so we also should walk in newness of life" (Romans 6:4 NKJV).

Here is what we need to understand and grasp about the new creation, it is in fact just that, a creation. It is something that God, the Father and Creator of all, created. This new birth that each of us experience was brought about by the will of God, as John tells us in John 1:13 NKJV, it is not inherited nor do we get to decide to recreate ourselves anew. Let's be clear here, God did not just simply clean up our old nature. He could have, but when have we read that God takes the easy way out without teaching us a valuable lesson? What God did do was to create something entirely unique and fresh. He created something from nothing, completely new, just as He did in creating the whole universe. Only God, the true Creator, could accomplish a feat such as that. No other known or unknown "god" can take credit for that.

The second part of 2 Corinthians 5:17 NKJV, "old things have passed away". What is this really telling us here? The "old" is referring to everything that is considered part of our old nature. What are some of the old natures? Lovers of sin, natural pride, passions and bad habits, bad attitudes, unnatural affections, and reliance on works. So, with the passing away, it is what we once loved that has passed away, especially our self-righteousness and self-justification. With the passing away, *the newness has come!* The wonderful part of this is the starting over, fresh and new. The new things (life) replace the old things (dead).

Many of the things that we did before Christ are no longer something we want to do after accepting Christ. However, you must know that this change may not be immediate so don't beat yourself up if you trip, stumble and fall. It happens to the best of us. The one thing to remember is to not allow yourself to be tricked into thinking that you cannot continue to live a free life if you do trip, stumble and fall. Ask God to forgive you and get back on track. Self-pity is a tool the enemy uses against us to make us feel sorry for ourselves. You are redeemed and are being sanctified every single day. What does this mean? It means that you are being made holy each day. The desire to sin becomes less and less. As you mature, even though you will still sin, that sinning will become less and less frequent. The apostle Paul knew all too well about our sinful flesh, and how it needs to die every day as we grow in Christ. He exclaims, "I die daily" (1 Corinthians 15:31 NKJV). We too must die to our flesh daily.

You must know, there is difference between continuing to live in sin, and to continuing to sin. You may ask, "What about those Christians who continue to sin?". Well, let me share with you that sinless perfection will never be reached in this life! I have a secret for you, no one is perfect. Surprise! So, consider this before you go ahead and tell that person at your job that they really aren't perfect! The Bible says, "Let the redeemed of the Lord say so" (Psalms 107:2 NKJV). You have been redeemed and you should not keep it to yourself. Share with others what God has done for you; that you are a new creation. God has wiped your slate clean allowing you to start all over again, fresh and new.

Here is the difference. When you are a new creation, you are no longer a slave to sin as you use to be. You have now been freed from sin and that sin no longer has power over you, "We know that our old self was crucified with him in order that the body of sin might be brought to nothing, so that we would no longer be enslaved to sin. 7 For one who has died has been set free from sin" (Romans 6:6-7 ESV). It's now your choice to count yourself "dead to sin but alive to God in Christ Jesus" or "let sin reign" (Romans 6:11-12). You have the power now to choose to be alive to God in Christ Jesus.

As a new Christian, a new creation, what does it really mean? It means that you are a person professing belief in Jesus as the Christ (Messiah), or a person that believes a religion based on teachings of Jesus as the Christ. However, the dictionary's definition falls short of truly communicating the biblical meaning of what a Christian is. As a new creation, you meet the Bible's true definition of a Christian.

New Creation: Quiz

1. What does 2 Corinthians 5:17 say?

2. If you are a Christian, do you remember, and what was the date you became a new creation?

3. Our old sinful _____ was _____ to the _____ with _____.

4. What are some of the old natures?

    a.

    b.

    c.

5. The Old things represents _____, and the New things represents _____.

6. Where is the scripture "I die daily" found?

7. In your own words, what does it mean "Let the redeemed of the Lord say so?"

8. We have been given a choice to be free or enslaved by sin (True or False).

9. We have no power to choose to be alive to God in Christ Jesus (True or False).

10. Everyone loves a new _____.

Notes to Self:

Be the Church

He said to them, "But who do you say that I am?" Simon Peter
answered and said, "You are the Christ, the Son of the living God."
Jesus answered and said to him, "Blessed are you, Simon Bar-Jonah,
for flesh and blood has not revealed this to you, but My Father who is
in heaven. And I also say you that you are Peter, and on this rock, I will
build my church, and the gates of Hell shall not prevail against it. And
I will give you the keys of the kingdom of heaven, and whatever you
bind on earth will be bound in heaven,
and whatever you loose on earth will be loosed in heaven.
(Matthew 16:15-19 English Standard Version)

Being the church, what does it really mean to be the church of Christ? Not in a denominational meaning, but in more of a "spiritual relationship to Christ" meaning. The day the church actually came alive was on the Day of Pentecost in Acts chapter 2:1-3 NKJV "And when the day of Pentecost was now come, they were all together in one place. 2 And suddenly there came from heaven a sound as of the rushing of a mighty wind, and it filled all the house where they were sitting. 3 And there appeared unto them tongues parting asunder, like as of fire; and it sat upon each one of them". This was the beginning of the first church, or the true starting of what we call the first church. Keep in mind, the Roman Catholic church was NOT and is NOT

the "first church" as many of the Catholic faith may
believe.

There is no record anywhere in the New Testament
showing where the following acts were performed by the
"first church": submitting to a pope, baptizing infants,
praying to Mary, observing the ordinances of baptism and
the Lord's Supper as sacraments, having a select
priesthood, venerating (a ritual act of devotion to) Mary,
passing on apostolic authority to successors of the apostles,
or praying to saints. These are Roman Catholic core
elements of faith and were not practiced by the New
Testament Church. Clearly study will show that the two are
not the same.

The one and only true and first church that we are to
emulate, follow, and model ourselves after, is that one
recorded in the New Testament (Acts 2). As a result of the
Holy Spirit falling upon those that were in the upper room
(Acts 2), this was a miraculous spreading of the Good
News of Jesus Christ. It had been ten days since Jesus
ascended back into heaven, Acts 1:9 NKJV "And when he
had said these things, as they were looking on, he was lifted
up, and a cloud took him out of their sight". The disciples
were instructed to go back and wait and pray for the
outpouring (indwelling) of the Holy Spirit. There were

about 120 people, along with Jesus' disciples in the upper room, an area above the living quarters used for hosting dinners and parties, no mention of whose house it belonged to. "When the day of Pentecost arrived, they were all together in one place. 2 And suddenly there came from heaven a sound like a mighty rushing wind, and it filled the entire house where they were sitting. 3 And divided tongues as of fire appeared to them and rested on each one of them. 4 And they were all filled with the Holy Spirit and began to speak in other tongues as the Spirit gave them utterance" Acts 2:1-4 NKJV.

When Jesus told Peter, "I will build my church" was a foretelling of what was going to happen once He sent the Holy Spirit back to earth to those that received Him. "But when the Helper comes, whom I will send to you from the Father, the Spirit of truth, who proceeds from the Father, he will bear witness about me. 27 And you also will bear witness, because you have been with me from the beginning" John 15:26-27 NKJV; "When the Spirit of truth comes, he will guide you into all the truth, for he will not speak on his own authority, but whatever he hears he will speak, and he will declare to you the things that are to come" John 16:13.

Many people that are a part of a denominational organization, believe that the church is the physical building in which they assemble. They could not be more wrong. The physical building is not a biblical understanding of the true meaning of the word church. In the Greek language, *ekklesia* is translated as "an assembly" or better yet, "called-out, from the world for God". Thayer and Smith. (1999). "Greek Lexicon entry for Ekklesia". "The NAS New Testament Greek Lexicon". The root meaning is not that of a physical building, but in fact, it is a body of believers, people. In the book of Romans, Paul refers to the church in their *house*, "Greet the church that is in their house" (Romans 16:5 ESV), not a church building. It was those that came and assembled together in one place. The church, the people, are the body of Christ, the church He is the head of, "And God placed all things under his feet and appointed him to be over everything for the church, which is his body, the fullness of him who fills everything in every way" (Ephesians 1:22-23 NKJV). So, when you hear the phrase, "The body of Christ" it is not a denomination as many may believe. It is in fact made up of all those that are believers in Christ Jesus from the day of Pentecost (Acts 2), and all those that have received Him today, until the day Christ returns.

If someone were to ask you what church do you attend, what would your answer be? Like most people, your answer would more than likely be that of a physical nature, identifying a building. But look at it in a different way; look at as you are being the physical building (church) that the Holy Spirit dwells in. Just as when Jesus entered the world, there was a physical body prepared for Him (Hebrews 10:5 NKJV), and through that body (Philippians 2:7 NKJV), He demonstrated the love of God, especially by His death on the cross which was a sacrificial type of love, it was clearly tangible and boldly done, "but God shows his love for us in that while we were still sinners, Christ died for us" Romans 5:8 NKJV. You can show this same type of tangible and bold love by sacrificially giving your all to and for Christ. You can be the *real church*.

Be the Church: Quiz

1. Who did Jesus say, "Upon this rock I will build my church" to?

2. Where is the Day of Pentecost found in the Bible?

3. What does *ekklesia* mean?

4. The "Body of Christ" is a denomination (True or False).

5. You must be in a physical building in order to be a part of the "body of Christ" (True or False).

6. The Roman Catholic church is recorded as the first church in the New Testament? (True or False).

7. The "body of Christ" are those that believe and follow Christ (True or False).

8. How many were said to be in the Upper Room?

9. How can you show the love of Christ?

10. What church do you attend?

Notes to Self:

The Holy Spirit

But you shall receive power when the Holy Spirit has come upon you;
and you shall be witnesses to Me in Jerusalem, and in all Judea and
Samaria, and to the end of the earth.
(Acts 1:8 NKJV)

Growing up in church I would always hear people talking and even teaching about the Holy Ghost. But as I got older, I heard more contemporary churches use the term Holy Spirit. Why the change? Some nontraditional churches had nerve to say that the term Holy Ghost was too spooky, so they started using the term Holy Spirit to draw more people. Seriously?

So, what is the difference between the Holy Ghost and the Holy Spirit? Over the years (and we are talking several hundred years), "Ghost" and "Spirit" has changed places. The King James Version is the only version that uses the "Holy Ghost" of the modern English translations of the Bible that uses the "Holy Ghost" today. If you were to look up and count how often the King James uses "Holy Ghost" you will see that it occurs 90 times and the "Holy Spirit" occurs 7 times. There really isn't a clear reason why those that translated the Bible, used Ghost more often than Spirit. In most instances, some of the recent translation of

Scripture, the word "Spirit" replaces "Ghost" (cf. Matthew 28:19; Acts 5:3-4; Acts 28:25-26; 1 Corinthians 12:4-6). No matter what term is used, the Holy Ghost is the active breath of God blowing where He desires.

What does it mean to be Filled? In the Bible says, "And I will pray the Father, and He will give you another Helper, that He may abide with you forever" (John 14:16 NKJV). Before Jesus left the disciples and ascended into heaven, he promised to send back a "helper" or "comforter" to dwell in all believers. The indwelling of the Holy Spirit is essential to the lives of those that are believers. It is a gift that takes place at the time of believing. Think of it as a down payment for future glorification in Jesus Christ, "who also has sealed us and given us the Spirit in our hearts as a guarantee" (2 Corinthians 1:22 NKJV). "And do not grieve the Holy Spirit of God, by whom you were sealed for the day of redemption" (Ephesians 4:30 NKJV).

When we hear and talk about the Holy Spirit, our attention is drawn to chapter 2 of the Book of Acts (also known as the Book of the Holy Spirit), on the Day of Pentecost, after the resurrection of Christ. But that is not the first time we hear of the Holy Spirit appearing to man. We read in the Gospel of Luke 1-2 NKJV that prior to the birth of Jesus, it was John the Baptist (Jesus' first cousin) that was filled with the Holy while still in his mother Elizabeth's womb, "For indeed, as soon as the voice of your greeting sounded in my ears, the babe leaped in my womb for joy" (Luke 1:44 NKJV).

Being filled with the Holy Spirit/Ghost, however one wants to say it, both refer to the Third Person of the Holy Trinity. Ah yes, the Trinity! In order to understand the Holy Spirit, one must know who the Holy Spirit is and what a very important role He plays in the life of a Christian.

The Bible is clear when it says there is only God (Deut. 6:4 NKJV; 1 Cor. 8:4; Gal. 3:20; 1 Tim. 2:5), however, as we study deeper into the word, we see that God actually is three separate and distinct individuals. This is one of the greatest mysteries known to man. How can one be three? How can there be one in the same? The simplest way to explain this phenomenon (and in a way that even a child could grasp and visualize its elementary meaning) is by using a subject that is usually not the favorite in school, chemistry. In this example, one can't help but to enjoy its simple lesson. The nature of water (H_2O) is one compound that can exist in three separate states; ice, liquid, and vapor. But they are all made of the two natural elements that form water. In reference to our God, this is not the complete picture, and does not invalidate His oneness, it's just a simple way to illustrate His three "persons". The Holy Spirit is an attribute of God.

God the Father, God the Son, and God the Holy Spirit. It is a unified Godhead that is known as the "Trinity" in Christianity. There is no earthly way for man to be able to comprehend and explain this mystery and the complexity of an infinite God. Our little, finite minds are not able to explain the heavenly, because our minds are earthly. All that we do and all that we see regarding the heavenly, is based on our faith. Even though we cannot understand why and how certain things are. Our faith is what we stand on in a faithless world (Hebrews 11:1, 3, 6 NKJV; 1 Corinthians 2:5-10, 14; 13:12).

We received God and the gift of His Spirit by faith (John 7:37-39 NKJV). The very moment you receive Christ into your heart, is the very moment the spirit of God dwells within you "In him you also, when you heard the word of truth, the gospel of your salvation, and believed in him, were sealed with the promised Holy Spirit" Ephesians 1:13 NKJV. In the following chapter we will discuss the Tongues and how it plays an important role in the lives of those that are saved and filled with the spirit of God (Acts 2:4).

The only way that man can know the things of God is if it is revealed by the Holy Spirit. The Holy Spirit is intelligent, He has emotions, and He has a will, "For who knows a person's thoughts except the spirit of that person, which is in him? So also no one comprehends the thoughts of God except the Spirit of God" (1 Corinthians 2:11 NKJV). The Holy Spirit has specific functions and roles in our lives for God, "When the Spirit of truth comes, he will guide you into all the truth, for he will not speak on his own authority, but whatever he hears he will speak, and he will declare to you the things that are to come" (John 16:13 NKJV). The one thing we will never have to worry about when it comes to the Holy Spirit is having the right things to say at the right time. The Holy Spirit gives us what to say, how to say it, and when to say it, "But the Helper, the Holy Spirit, whom the Father will send in my name, he will teach you all things and bring to your remembrance all that I have said to you" (John 14:26 NKJV).

At the end of the book of Matthew, the disciples were given special instructions by Jesus, ones that would change the world forever as they knew it. Jesus said, "Go ye therefore, and make disciples of all the nations, baptizing them into the name of the Father, and of the Son and of the Holy Spirit" (Matthew 28:19 NKJV). This commission was not only for the disciples of that day, but for all those that follow Christ today. Are you filled with the spirit of God? Are you making disciples of others?

Names and Titles of the Holy Spirit:

Below are a few of the many names for which the Holy Spirit is known. They denote many of the functions and aspects of His ministry:

a) Comforter / Counselor / Helper / Advocate: (Isaiah 11:2 NKJV; John 14:16; 15:26; 16:7)

b) Intercessor: (Romans 8:26 NKJV)

c) Author: (2 Peter 1:21 NKJV; 2 Timothy 3:16)

d) The Lord / Spirit of God / Christ: (Matthew 3:16 NKJV; 2 Corinthians 3:17; 1 Peter 1:11)

e) Spirit of Truth: (John 14:17; 16:13; 1 Corinthians 2:12-16 NKJV)

f) Witness: (Romans 8:16 NKJV; Hebrews 2:4; 10:15)

g) Spirit of Life: (Romans 8:2 NKJV)

h) Teacher: (John 14:26 NKJV; 1 Corinthians 2:13)

The Holy Spirit: Quiz

1. The term Ghost has been changed to what term today?

2. Name the Godhead Trinity.

3 What are some of the name/titles of the Holy Spirit?

4. The Book of Acts is also known as the Book of the

_____,

5. How are heavenly things revealed to man?

6. In reference to being able to speak up at the right time, who gives of the power to speak the right things at the right time?

7. How was John the Baptist related to Jesus?

8. Who was John the Baptist's mother?

9. What was Jesus' commission to the disciples before He left earth?

10. Are you filled with the Spirit of God?

Notes to Self:

Tongues

And these signs will follow those who believe: In My name they will
cast out demons;
they will speak with new tongues;
(Mark 16:17 NKJV)

Speaking in tongues is the ability (gift) to speak in a language (an unknown language or heavenly language) other than your own at a time when God's spirit moves upon you.

The introduction of tongues is first seen in the Book of Acts, or the Book of the Holy Spirit, on the Day of Pentecost (Acts 2:1-4 NKJV). This was the very first occurrence of the any such event. After the 120, including the disciples of Jesus, all were assembled together and praying, in the upper room, an area used for banquets and weddings, of a house borrowed by the disciples. The Bible says, "And suddenly there came a sound from heaven as of a rushing mighty wind, and it filled all the house where they were sitting. 3 And there appeared unto them cloven tongues like as of fire, and it sat upon each of them. 4 And they were all filled with the Holy Ghost, and began to speak with other tongues, as the Spirit gave them utterance" (Acts 2:2-4 NKJV).

In the Greek, tongues are translated as *languages*, which should bring a better understanding as to why it is called tongues. Speaking in tongues was considered a miracle since the people filled with the gift were Hebrew and had no formal training in other languages, "And they were all amazed and marveled, saying one to another, 'Behold, are not all these which speak Galileans? And how hear we every man in our own tongue, wherein we were born... the wonderful works of God?'" (Acts 2:7-11).

Growing up in church it was believed that to be filled with the Holy Spirit, one must speak in tongues. This type of teaching came with the following question, "was one not filled with the Holy Spirit if they did not speak in tongues after they were saved?" The speaking in tongues during the time of the Apostles was for the benefit of those that did not know of Christ and what He did while he was on earth. The ability to speak in another language to a person in their native language, was indeed a gift from God in order to declare His mighty works. It was for the benefit of the one hearing the message of God in their native tongue with no interpreter needed. It was needed to edify the church. Paul said, "Now, brothers, if I come to you speaking in tongues, how will I benefit you unless I bring you some revelation or knowledge or prophecy or teaching?" (1 Corinthians

14:6 English Standard Version). In other words, what benefit is it to those that do not know what is being said in unless it's in their own language? Therefore, it is called a gift of interpreting tongues. The person speaking the message of God can then be understood by someone who has been given the gift to interpret to those listening, "Do all possess gifts of healing? Do, all speak with tongues? Do all interpret?" (1 Cor. 12:30 ESV). There is no confusing this, if God is going to use someone to speak for Him then He will give the gift to someone to interpret His message, "For this reason anyone who speaks in a tongue should pray that he may interpret what he says" (1 Cor. 14:13 ESV).

Some religions may think that the gift of tongues have ceased and tongues do not seem to occur today in the same manner as did in the New Testament (1 Cor. 13:8-12), God is still performing these miracles today (1 Cor. 1:7). True, it may not be as prevalent as when the Holy Spirit fell on the Day of Pentecost, however, God is still God and His Spirit still moves in a great way. Man changes, not God. Do not believe the hype, that the speaking of tongues is no longer needed in the church, "For God is not a God of confusion but of peace. As in all the churches of the saints" (1 Cor. 12:11 ESV).

The Jehovah Witness teachings claim tongues have ceased mainly because "tongues were passed on to other Christians in the presence of the apostles, usually by the apostles by placing their hands on them" (Acts 8: 18; 10:44-46 ESV). "It appears that those who received the gifts of the spirit from the apostles did not transfer them to others" (Acts 8: 5-7, 14-17). This is their illustration: "a government official may issue a driver's license to someone, but that person is not given the legal authority to issue a license to anyone else. Apparently, speaking in tongues ended with the death of the apostles and those who had personally received the gift from them." (JW.ORG). These claims are false. For one, speaking in tongues did not die with the apostles, and two, the apostles did not give their followers the gift of speaking in tongues. The Bible is very clear in how this gift was given, "And these signs will accompany (follow) those who believe... they will speak in new tongues" (Mark 16:17 NIV). If the tongues died when the apostles died, then how is it that many today are being given this spiritual gift? If you believe, you too can be gifted with speaking in tongues. This is one way that God audibly speaks to the church today. The Jehovah Witness teachings also claim, "The miraculous gift of speaking in tongues evidently ended about the end of the first century

C.E. *No one today* [emphasis added] can rightly claim to speak in tongues by God's power." (JW.ORG) This statement is unfounded and false.

Therefore, studying the word of God is imperative and is being led by His spirit into all truth. It is very easy to be misled if you are not in His word and praying for the Holy Spirit to reveal to you what is right and true. "Study to shew thyself approved unto God, a workman that needeth not to be ashamed, rightly dividing the word of truth" (2 Timothy 2:15 KJV). There are many that believe speaking in tongues have ceased, "Love never fails. But where there are prophecies, they will cease; where there are tongues, they will be still; whether there be knowledge, it will pass away" (1 Cor. 13:8 NIV). Even some Christian leaders today are teaching that speaking in tongues has ceased. Where in the word of God does it prove, without a shadow of doubt, that the Gift that God gives and keeps on giving, has ceased? Yes, there will be a time when all of what was written regarding this scripture will cease, but that time has not come yet come because Christ has not returned. As long as there will be sinners, the gift of speaking will continue. It was for this reason the gift of tongues was given, "In the Law it is written: 'With other tongues and through the lips of foreigners I will speak to this people, but even then they will not listen to me, says the Lord.' 22 Tongues, then, are a sign, not for believers but for unbelievers; prophecy, however, is not for unbelievers but for believers" (1 Cor. 14:21-22 NIV).

Our society has become more and more wicked, thus causing the moving of God to be less and less amongst His people. In the Bible, sin was the cause of God's silence. And if our world does not take heed to those same warnings, we too will lose the voice of God. There were times when even David felt that God was distant, "Why, Lord, do you stand far off? Why do you hide yourself in times of trouble?" (Psalm 10:1 NIV). However, David realized that God was still with him, "You, Lord, hear the desire of the afflicted; you encourage them, and you listen to their cry" (v.17).

There is so much to be said regarding the use of tongues and how the idea of tongues is being misused today, simply because of constant erring in certain Christian circles. The Holy Spirit was given for two reasons, one to edify the Body of Christ and two to glorify God. Speaking in tongues is not a necessary sign of salvation as mentioned in the Bible. Instead, salvation is achieved by grace through faith, "For by grace are ye saved through faith; and that not of yourselves: *it is* the gift of God" (Ephesians 2:8 KJV). Yes, there were those in the early church that spoke in tongues the moment they became Christians, but not all spoke because God does not give the gift of tongues to everyone (Acts 2:4; 10:46; 19:6 KJV). Remember what Paul wrote to the Corinthian church in 1 Cor. 12:4-11, 28-31 NIV, many of the early Christians had received the gift of tongues and did not really understand how it was properly used when gathered together. The tongues were a gift from God to those that believed, and to aid in the building and edifying of the Body of Christ, which is... the Church.

So, even though a sign for salvation is not speaking in tongues, speaking in tongues is indeed a sign, as in fruit of the Spirit (Galatians 5:22-23 NKJV). When it comes to speaking in tongues, there are three types of divisions in the use of speaking in tongues: First, there is the private prayer language that you use to pray, while laying before God in your private prayer time (in your prayer closet). This type of prayer language is not interpreted. The prayer closet is a place where you can really open yourself up to God and cry out to Him in private. It's where you can talk and spiritually strategize against the enemy. In the natural, wars are fought and won on the battlefield, in the spiritual, wars are fought and won in prayer, inside your *war room*. (as an aside the movie War Room is highly recommended).

Second, the tongue that is interpreted, is defined as proper usage within the church. For example, when the spirit of God falls upon a person in a church setting and they begin to speak in God's heavenly language, God then provides another to interpret what He has spoken. But there are times when there may be no one present to interpret and the person speaking in tongues interprets God's message. That's the gift of interpretation in affect. And third, there is the tongue of missionary context. This appears in the word during evangelism, just as in the New Testament, where people are presenting the gospel to those that speak another language, and they hear God's message in their own native tongue. It was appropriate during the time of the apostles because as they ministered to outer regions, they had to be able to share the gospel in other languages. Thus, the gift of speaking in tongues was very prominent in the New Testament and it is still very prominent today.

Every true believer of Christ should want and desire to be filled in such a way that they are overcome with the spirit of God and able to speak in tongues. It's a language that you can practice in your prayer closet. The more you speak in your heavenly language the more you will be used to doing so. It's a language the devil cannot understand and will be unable to eavesdrop on your petitioning to God. The gift of speaking in tongues is yours for the asking; ask and speak with the tongues of heaven.

Tongues: Quiz

1. When did "tongues" first appear to man?

2. In the Greek, tongues are translated as

_____.

3. To be filled with the Holy Spirit one must speak in tongues? (True or False).

4. The gift of tongues has ceased today? (True or False).

5. What are two reasons mentioned that the Holy Spirit was given?

    a.

    b.

6. How are you saved, according to the Bible? (Eph. 2:8)

7 What are the three different types of tongues used?

    a.

    b.

    c.

8. What is the importance of speaking in tongues?

9. What are the Jehovah Witnesses beliefs in reference to the Gift of Tongues?

10. Have you spoken in tongues? Do you believe it is important to do so?

Notes to Self:

Heaven

In the beginning, God created the heavens and the earth
(Genesis 1:1 ESV).

*In my Father's house are many rooms. If it were not so, would I have
told you that I go to prepare a place for you?* (John 14:2 ESV).

Heaven! According to the American Heritage Dictionary, (2011). Heaven is defined as, "the abode of God, the angels, and the spirits of the righteous after death; the place of state of existence of the blessed after the mortal life."

Q: What is heaven?

A: It is the dwelling place of God

The word heaven is said to be found in the New Testament 276 times. Now that would be a great homework assignment for you to find, in the scriptures, the word *heaven*. Did you know that there is, in fact, more than one heaven? If you are a new Christian this may be news to you, but if you have read and studied any of the apostle Paul's writing then you would remember him saying that he was "caught up to the third heaven" (2 Corinthians 12:2a ESV). Paul said he was caught up to the third heaven, so it must mean that there are a couple more existing heavens.

The third heaven, where God abodes, is referred to as "heaven of heavens" in Nehemiah 9:6. In reading the first book of the Bible (Genesis) it is possible that the first heaven is referred to as the "sky" or translated as the "firmament" containing the clouds, and birds, "let the...fowl that may fly above the earth in the open firmament of heaven (Genesis 1:20 NKJV)". The interstellar (outer space), where the planets, stars, and many other celestial objects exist, is considered the second heaven, (Genesis 1:14-20).

Have you ever wondered if heaven was indeed a real place? There are many movies and books written by those that have claimed they have died and gone to heaven, but not only that, they came back! My question (as well as many others) is, "why would you come back?". Books like, Heaven is for Real by Todd Burpo; In Light of Eternity by Randy Alcorn; Heaven by Randy Alcorn; The Slumber of Christianity by Ted Dekker; Heaven: My Father's House by Anne Graham Lotz; The Five People You Meet in Heaven by Mitch Albom; 90 Minutes in Heaven by Don Piper; and I'll Hold You in Heaven by Jack Hayford, these are rated as the top books about heaven (Fairchild, Mary 2018).

Let me ask you this, if you died and went to heaven, would you want to return to this place? I think not. If heaven is as beautiful as claimed (which I do not doubt) by those that say they have been there, then why would they come back? Or, maybe it's for us to learn from the personal experience of those that have died, gone to heaven, and have returned; that there really is a heaven? You would think that just trusting in what the Bible says about heaven is enough to believe that there is a place called heaven. In an article *What is Heaven Live?* Rev. Charles Ball said, "Heaven is a place, just as much a place as is New York or Chicago". (1998).

Q: What is Heaven?

A: Heaven is a place of fellowship and eternal joy.

In the Bible we read that the throne of God is in fact heaven, Isaiah 66:1 ESV "Thus says the LORD: 'Heaven is my throne, and the earth is my footstool; what is the house that you would build for me, and what is the place of my rest?'"; Acts 7:48-49 NKJV "Yet the Most High does not dwell in houses made by hands, as the prophet says, 49 'Heaven is my throne, and the earth is my footstool. What kind of house will you build for me, says the Lord, or what is the place of my rest?'"; Matthew 5:34-35 NKJV "But I say to you, Do not take an oath at all, either by heaven, for it is the throne of God, 35 or by the earth, for it is his footstool, or by Jerusalem, for it is the city of the great King".

When Jesus ascended back to heaven (Acts 1:9-12 ESV), He entered into heaven itself, not one made by hands, or a man-made copy of a sanctuary to look like heaven (Hebrews 9:24 ESV). Jesus' heavenly ministry is serving on our behalf as our high priest. In the one and only true tabernacle that was made by God Himself, (Hebrews 6:19-20; 8:1-2 ESV). Some of the most quoted verses, especially during funerals is John 14:1-4 ESV, "Let not your hearts be troubled. Believe in God; believe also in me. 2 In my Father's house are many rooms. If it were not so, would I have told you that I go to prepare a place for you? 3 And if I go and prepare a place for you, I will come again and will take you to myself, that where I am you may be also. 4 And you know the way to where I am going". Jesus was preparing His disciples for His departure; they were sad in heart and in spirit. He was in fact encouraging them not to be sad because He would no longer be with them on earth. But He was going away to prepare a glorious place for them to be with Him when He returned (John 14:3 ESV). Amazing how these verses are favorite readings for funerals today, for Christians and non-Christians alike.

All the events leading up to this point in <u>John 14 ESV</u> Jesus has been teaching, instructing, healing the sick, raising the dead and preparing them for His upcoming death. The disciples were confused as to why He had to go and leave them behind, and why they could not follow Him. In consoling them He revealed a greater understanding of Himself. Can you imagine hanging out with a friend, being mentored for three and a half years, learning how to be successful in all areas of life only to have them up and tell you that they are leaving, by way of death, but not to be troubled because he would come back? Your thoughts would be confused and complexed as well. Jesus told His disciples, "Let not let you heart be troubled" (<u>John 14:1 NJKV</u>). This is the love of a Good Shepherd. He is comforting His sheep who are troubled in their hearts. What better way to say *you can trust me?* When He said, "You believe in God, believe also in Me". This was the solution to their troubled hearts of Him leaving them behind. What better way to say, "you can trust me?". Though Jesus was not going to be with them, He assured them that whatever He told them in the past three and a half years together, He was going to accomplish it.

How in the world could the disciples continue the work without Jesus with them? They were fearful and perplexed in their hearts, their Lord and Savior was soon to leave them. Here are parts of the conversations and questions they had with Jesus (John 14 NJKV):

Thomas: "We do not know why you are going; how can we know the way?" (v.5).

Jesus: "I am the way, the truth, and the life. No one comes to the Father except through Me" (v.6).

Philip: "Show us the Father, that is sufficient" (v.8).

Jesus: "Have I been with you so long, and yet you have not known Me, Phillip? He who has seen Me has seen the Father" (v.9).

Q: Where is heaven?

A: Heaven is wherever God is.

The disciples wanted to know what was going on and why? Thomas was upset about what was happening and not knowing the way "How can we know the way, if we don't know where you are going?" That night, there was just no understanding how they were going to do anything without Jesus being present. His work on earth was done, He was finished, and it was time for Him to leave and go back to the place from which He came, heaven. The word of God is still comforting our hearts today, reminding us not to be troubled in all that is going in this world because someday the return of Christ will be worth it. Since the beginning of time and the fall, of man we have been yearning and longing to return home to our Creator. Just like Jesus, this is not our home and the inner man desires to be with God. The amazing thing about all of this is that most Americans (at least 82%) that believe that there is a heaven, truly expect to go there when they die, according to Pew Research Center's 2014 Religious Landscape Study, and yet many of them really don't want to die right now to get there. People want to go to heaven but do not want to live a life guaranteeing their safe passage there. The Bible is very clear in instructing us how to, and by whom, we need to go through, in order to get to heaven.

Here's some help just in case you need it. Jesus said that He was the only true way to the Father, "No one comes to the Father, except through Me" (John 14:6 NIV). That pretty much settles any other claims that may say otherwise. Our citizenship is, in fact, in heaven. Paul affirms this in his letter to the Philippian church, "But our citizenship is in heaven. And we eagerly await a Savior from there, the Lord Jesus Christ," (Philippians 3:20 NIV). It is our hope, as believers, to make heaven our new home, Paul wrote, "the faith and love that spring from the hope stored up for you in heaven and about which you have

already heard in the true message of the gospel"
(Colossians 1:5).

We have all heard, *to be absent from the body is to be present with the Lord.* It is paraphrased from, "Therefore we are always confident, knowing that, whilst we are at home in the body, we are absent from the Lord: 7 (For we walk by faith, not by sight:) 8 Yes, we are of good courage, and we would rather be away from the body and at home with the Lord. 9 So whether we are at home or away, we make it our aim to please him" (2 Corinthians 5:6-9 ESV). This is and should be our one and only focus and goal in this life; to one day see God face to face in our new home, heaven.

Heaven: Quiz

1. Do you believe that there is a place called heaven?

2. Who made heaven?

3. Where is it found in the Bible?

4. Where is it found in the Bible that there are many mansions in heaven?

5. What is the only way we can get to the Father in heaven?

6. Where is our true "citizenship" located?

7. What is heaven?

8. Where is heaven?

9. How many times is heaven found in the New Testament?

10. What is, and should be our focus and goal in life as Christians?

Notes to Self:

Hell

And fear not them which kill the body but are not able to kill the soul:
but rather fear him which is able to destroy both soul and body in hell.
(Matthew 10:28 New King James Version)

"Go to hell!" Ever heard that being spewed out of the mouth of an irate individual? Or maybe that irate person was you. Ever told someone to go to hell? Let's be very clear here, as real as heaven is, make no mistake, hell is just as real! Hell is a real place, so when you get mad and tell people to go to hell, it's exceptionally bad. Never once have I heard anyone tell someone to go to heaven. Why not? Because all that we hear about heaven is how lovely, peaceful, and what beautiful a place it is. Hell, on the other hand is depicted by sheer anguish and pain, sorrow and grief. Being told to go to hell means that they really want you to suffer in a place of conscious and continuous torment.

Amazingly enough, despite the clear teachings of heaven and hell, there are people who believe in heaven's reality while rejecting the reality of hell. Wishful thinking! The Bible declares the reality of hell, "And death and hell were cast into the lake of fire. This is the second death. 15

And whosoever was not found written in the book of life was cast into the lake of fire" Revelation 20:14-15 NKJV. And John writes, "And I saw a new heaven and a new earth: for the first heaven and the first earth were passed away; and there was no more sea. 2 And I John saw the holy city, new Jerusalem, coming down from God out of heaven, prepared as a bride adorned for her husband" Revelation 21:1-2 NKJV. Did you not know that Jesus spent more of His time warning the people of the perils of hell then He did in encouraging people with the hope of heaven? Amazing. Apparently, it was very important in His earthly ministry. He did not want to lose not one soul, hence His coming to die on the cross.

Hades is Greek for the Hebrew word *sheol* (place of the dead). Hell is translated ten times in the Bible and grave is translated only once, "O death, where is your sting? O grave, where is your victory?" (1 Corinthians 15:55 KJV). Hell is translated from the Greek word Gehenna (Hebrew valley of Hinnom). Hell means a place of everlasting torment (Matthew 10:28) for the loss of unsaved souls. Hell was never intended for humans. It was created for Satan and his fallen angels (spiritual demonic beings) for rebelling against God and so, were casted out of heaven "How you are fallen from heaven, O Day Star, son of

Dawn! How you are cut down to the ground, you who laid the nations low!" (Isaiah 14:12 ESV). It must have been extremely quick when Satan, and those who were deceived by him, were kicked out of heaven because even Jesus said, "I saw Satan fall like a lightning from heaven" (Luke 10:18 ESV). And in Revelation 9:1 KJV Satan is seen as "a star that had fallen from the sky to earth". Just imagine a star shooting across the sky; now picture it being Satan falling from grace to the earth. But here is a theological mind binding fact, "And death and hell were cast into the lake of fire. This is the second death. 15 And whosoever was not found written in the book of life was cast into the lake of fire" (Revelation 20:14-15 KJV). This takes the subject of hell to a whole other level.

The Five "I Wills" of Satan and his Fall from Grace: Isaiah 14:13-14 KJV

1. I WILL ASCEND INTO HEAVEN
2. I WILL EXALT MY THRONE ABOVE THE STARS OF GOD
3. I WILL SIT ALSO UPON THE MOUNT OF THE CONGREGATION
4. I WILL ASCEND ABOVE THE HEIGHTS OF THE CLOUDS
5. I WILL BE LIKE THE MOST HIGH

Pride = Fall

1. P - Position
2. R - Rule
3. I - Idolized
4. D - Dominion
5. E - Equality

The fall was all based on this one word, "PRIDE". It's the fall of every person that is driven by power and a will to take over. The Bible says that, "Pride goes before destruction, a haughty spirit before a fall" (Proverbs 16:18 NIV). Look at every person in power that was prideful, and you will find that their end results were not too good. In every single case they fell, and great was that fall. Pride is cancerous and has, for centuries, destroyed kingdoms and empires. Pride has caused men to divorce their spouses and walk away from their family. It has ruined friendships and caused more conflicts with nations, causing more wars. Even though pride can have a negative outcome if not controlled, it too can have a positive outcome if used properly. For instance, if God has blessed you through your faithfulness with a brand-new house, there is nothing wrong in being proud of that house and taking good care of that house because you realize it was a gift and blessing from God.

If you are a new Christian, be proud of the fact that you were one of the ones that God chose. Your one desire should be to one day reign with Christ in heaven. Your one goal in life is living to please your heavenly Father. What does that look like? How can you live a life that is pleasing to God? Well, to start with, find yourself in His word daily. If you don't read the instruction manual, you will never know what is expected of you. Reading the word of God is our way of hearing God speak to us personally. The Bible is filled with love letters written to His children. There are letters of discipline and letters of instructions on how to live a pleasing life while here on earth. A wonderfully written book by the apostle Paul addresses living a life pleasing to God, "Finally, then, brethren, we urge and exhort in the Lord Jesus that you should abound more and more, just as you received from us how you ought to walk and to please God" (1 Thessalonians 4:1 NKJV).

Does God send people to hell? This is a question that many have asked for thousands of years. "If God is so loving, why would God send people to hell?" God does not send anyone to hell! That needs to be repeated, *God does not send anyone to hell!* This is the choice of every created being on earth. And it is a free choice. You do not have to go to hell. But you may ask, "How does one choose to go to hell?" The simplest way to answer this question is, *by not choosing to follow the pathway of Christ*. People go to hell because of their own sin, this is free choice (a will) we have been given by God. He allows us to choose whatever path we want. Choose wisely my child.

Hell was not created for us (mankind) it was originally created for Satan and those angels that rebelled against God. "Then he will say to those on his left, 'Depart from me, you cursed, into the eternal fire prepared for the devil and his angels'" (Matthew 25:41 ESV). Mankind goes to hell for the same reason the fallen angels went to hell, for sin, "for all have sinned and fall short of the glory of God" (Romans 3:23 ESV). All because of the sin of Adam, mankind has a sinful nature, "Therefore, just as sin came into the world through one man, and death through sin, and so death spread to all men because all sinned..." (Romans 5:12 ESV). Hell is also referred to as "darkness" and to be real, any place where God isn't, is certainly dark, "Then said the king to the servants, bind him hand and foot, and take him away, and cast him into outer darkness, there shall be weeping and gnashing of teeth" (Matthew 22:13 KJV).

There is good news. Because God is so loving and forgiving, He has made a way for mankind to avoid hell, and that's by accepting and trusting in the atonement of His

Son, Christ Jesus. By Jesus coming to earth to atone for the sins of man, the punishment of hell has been removed, "Whoever believes and is baptized will be saved, but whoever does not believe will be condemned" (Mark 16:16 ESV). Jesus bore the weight of the whole world's sin upon Himself, "He himself bore our sins in his body on the tree, that we might die to sin and live to righteousness. By his wounds you have been healed" (1 Peter 2:24 ESV). If you have accepted Christ into your heart and you truly believe that you have been forgiven from the stain of sin and recused from the punishment that comes from dying with your sins, then going to hell should never enter your mind. And because of this sacrificial and merciful love of Jesus, we have a free pathway to Christ; away from hell.

Hell: Quiz

1. What is the Greek translation of Hebrew word sheol?

2. What is the Greek translation word for hell?

3. How was Satan's fall from heaven described?

4. What are the five "I Wills" of Satan, and where are they found?

    a.

    b.

    c.

    d.

    e.

5. What is the acronym for pride?

    a.

    b.

    c.

    d.

    e.

6. Why was hell created?

7. Do you believe there is a hell? Yes / No (Explain your answer)

8. How does one go to hell?

9. What/who is our pathway to God?

10. What is the second death? (Rev. 20:14)

Notes to Self:

Sin

Whoever commits sin also commits lawlessness, and sin is lawlessness.
(1 John 3:4 NKJV)

Sin, such a small word that has such huge life altering impact. Sin is the one thing that can separate us from our heavenly Father. It was the one thing that got Adam and Eve banded and kicked out of the garden of Eden, "therefore the LORD God sent him out from the garden of Eden to work the ground from which he was taken. 24 He drove out the man, and at the east of the garden of Eden he placed the cherubim and a flaming sword that turned every way to guard the way to the tree of life" (Genesis 3:23-24 ESV). And because of this sin, we all suffer the consequences.

Sin, what is it? Sin is transgression against the laws of God. It is anything that displeases God. Breaking His laws. Disobedience. Rebellion. Throughout the journey of the children of Israel, they rebelled against God, "Remember! Do not forget how you provoked the Lord your God to wrath in the wilderness. From the day that you departed from the land of Egypt until you came to this place, you have been rebellious against the Lord" (Deuteronomy 9:7 NKJV).

There is a study of sin called the Hamartiology Theology. It is investigation of the origination of sin and how it affects mankind, the degrees of sin and the many different types of sin, as well as the results of sin. No one really knows the basic origin of sin or how it manifested, in all places, heaven. But we do read that as a result of it, Lucifer (now called Satan), was kicked out of heaven for his rebellious pride (Isaiah 14:13-14 NKJV). He was actually on earth before man was created (Luke 1:18 NKJV). He had to have seen how God loved His creation, Adam was perfect in every way. That had to have infuriated Satan and since his fall from grace (heaven), he has been scheming and plotting of ways to get back at God and deceive as many people as he can before he is cast into the *lake of fire forever*, "The devil who had deceived them was cast into the lake of fire and brimstone, where the beast and the false prophet are; and they shall be tormented day and night for ever and ever" (Revelation 20:10 NKJV). Isn't it amazing that we all know what the devil's end will be, and yet he is still working overtime to deceive people?

The Scheme: Temptation, The Fall of Man (Genesis 3 NKJV)

In Genesis chapter 3 we are introduced to the serpent, Satan, in fallen form. It is where Satan crafted his plan to deceive man. And it is in the form of what we call temptation. He twisted the truth of God, and even today that same sin is used to deceive mankind. Satan tricks people into thinking that a lie is really the truth "Has God indeed said, 'You shall not eat of every tree of the garden'?" (Gen. 3:3b; Gen. 2:16-17). This one question enticed Eve to doubt. Her doubt was then planted into the heart of her husband, Adam; the one God created first, the one that could have stopped it all and rebuked his wife for bringing this enticing thought of doubt. One can only try to imagine what life would be like if Adam would have refused to eat the fruit from the tree of the knowledge of good and evil (Gen. 2:16). And just as God warned them, if they did eat of that tree, they would "surely die" (Gen. 2:17). It wasn't a natural death as one would think, and that's the twisted part of Satan's lie. The fact was that they would not die but they would be as wise as God, "For God knows that when you eat of it your eyes will be opened, and you will be like God, knowing good and evil" (Gen. 3:5 ESV). This was what convinced Eve to eat the fruit. Curiosity! Is this why secrets can't be kept today? We must know what is forbidden.

The death came, not in the natural sense but in a spiritual sense. That first sin caused man to be separated from God spiritually and because of man's sin, God placed a curse on all of mankind. He asked Adam, "Why?" he blamed the woman, He asked the woman, "Why?" and she blamed the serpent (Gen. 3:11-13 NKJV). The serpent had no one else to blame, so the LORD God said to the serpent, "Because you have done this, You *are* cursed more than all cattle, And more than every beast of the field; On your belly you shall go (this was the birth of the snake), And you shall eat dust All the days of your life" (Gen. 3:14 NKJV). It was promised that the seed of woman, one day, would save humanity from eternal damnation from the consequences of their sin, "And I will put enmity Between you and the woman, And between your seed and her Seed; He shall bruise your head, And you shall bruise His heel" (Gen. 3:14-15 NKJV). But until Jesus was born, earthly consequences of man's sin temporarily remained.

God removed Adam and Eve from the garden, knowing that if He did not, they just might eat of the tree of life and causing them to live forever, "Then the LORD God said, 'Behold, the man has become like one of Us, to know good and evil. And now, lest he put out his hand and take also of the tree of life, and eat, and live forever'— 23 therefore the

L ORD God sent him out of the garden of Eden to till the ground from which he was taken. 24 So He drove out the man; and He placed a cherubim at the east of the garden of Eden, and a flaming sword which turned every way, to guard the way to the tree of life" (Gen. 3:22-24 NKJV). Not only were Adam and Eve kicked out of the garden of Eden, they were prevented from ever returning to a perfect place they once knew.

Let's be very clear in our understanding of sin and how all sin has its consequences. Even though there may be degrees of sin (and some sins may be more detestable to God), they are all equally the same when it comes to the eternal consequences of sin and are punishable by death. Paul made this point evident when he wrote, "For the wages of sin *is* death, but the gift of God *is* eternal life in Christ Jesus our Lord" (Romans 6:23 NKJV). Sin carries with it, condemnation and eternal death in the lake of fire! "For all who do such things, all who behave unrighteous, *are* an abomination to the L ORD your God" (Deuteronomy 25:16 NKJV). You probably didn't know that God, in fact, hates. Yes, it's true. God hates. There are 117 references in the Bible of the word abomination (see references).

Six things the Lord hates:

1. Proud look (Proverbs 16:18 NKJV; Daniel 4:37; Jeremiah 50:31; Matthew 23:12)

2. Lying tongue (John 8:44 NKJV; John 8:32)

3. Murder (Exodus 20:13 NKJV; 1 John 3:15; Jeremiah 18:18)

4. Heart that devises wicked (Matthew 5:28 NKJV; Romans 6:23)

5. Feet that are swift in running to evil (Psalms 1:1 NKJV)

6. One who sows discord among brethren (Ephesians 4:31 NKJV; James 1:26)

Adam allowed and caused a great curse to fall upon all humanity yet to be born. A true fellowship was broken as a result of being enticed to disobey God. For centuries the world has been groaning and crying for natural and spiritual relief, a relief that ultimately will come through the redemptive love of Christ's return, "For we know that the whole creation has been groaning together in the pains of childbirth until now. 23 And not only the creation, but we ourselves, who have the first fruits of the Spirit, groan inwardly as we wait eagerly for adoption as sons, the redemption of our bodies" (Romans 8:22-23 ESV).

As a result of Christ coming to earth, being crucified, dying on a cross, being buried in a grave, only to rise again on third day, the "fallen" man has redemption of his sin, through the shed blood of Jesus Christ. All things, as we know of today, that are being destroyed by sin, will be restored by God upon Christ's return (Acts 3:21 NKJV). God said in His word that He would create a new heaven and a new earth, "For behold, I create new heavens and a new earth, and the former things shall not be remembered or come into mind" (Isaiah 65:17 ESV). Peter wrote, "waiting for and hastening the coming of the day of God, because of which the heavens will be set on fire and dissolved, and the heavenly bodies will melt as they burn! 13 But according to his promise we are waiting for new heavens and a new earth in which righteousness dwells" (2 Peter 3:12-13 ESV). John witnessed in his vision, "Then I saw a new heaven and a new earth, for the first heaven and the first earth had passed away, and the sea was no more" (Revelation 21:1 ESV).

You too, can *count yourself dead to sin and alive to God in Christ Jesus if you are born again*, "So you also must consider yourselves dead to sin and alive to God in Christ Jesus" (Revelation 6:11 ESV). You too, can be free of your sin (Romans 10:9-10 ESV).

Sin: Quiz

1. What is sin?

2. What is the study of the origination of sin called?

3. Satan was called_____, before his fall from heaven.

4. The first sin in the world was due to Satan _____ Eve.

5. What happened when Adam and Eve ate of the fruit of the knowledge of good and evil?

6. What was man's punishment for eating the fruit? (Genesis 3:23):

7. Satan (the serpent form) was turned into what for deceiving man?

8. What are the six things that God hates? (Proverbs 6:16-19):

    a.
    b.
    c.
    d.
    e.
    f.

9. What is an abomination?

10. How can one be made free of sin? (Romans 10:9-10):

Notes to Self:

Salvation

And they said, "Believe in the Lord Jesus, and you will be saved, you and your household.
(Acts 16:31 ESV)

What is salvation? We hear the talk of salvation every single Sunday of the month in church. But what is salvation, really? How can one obtain salvation? What is the "Plan of salvation" we hear about so often? Well, I am glad you asked because that is what we are going to be discussing in this lesson. I remember my days in Sunday School singing the salvation song. It went something like this, "Oh you can't get to hea-ven with-out it, S.A.L.V.A.T.I.O.N." It would have to be spelled it out. Everyone would stop singing except the person that was chosen at random, (which would be me most of the time), by the Sunday School Superintendent to spell out the word *salvation*. It was really embarrassing if you didn't know how to spell salvation. So, the song was a great way to learn how to spell salvation. But once we learned how to spell it, we would then learn what salvation really meant.

What is Salvation?

The dictionary defines salvation as, "preservation or deliverance from harm, ruin, or loss" (New Dictionary of Cultural Literacy). It's a lifeline, preservation, or conservation. In theology it's, *deliverance from sin and its consequences, believed by Christians to be brought about by faith in Christ.* It's redemption, saving, deliverance, reclamation, help.

The deliverance from suffering and danger, protect and save; that is salvation. It is often used in reference to spiritual deliverance. According to the Bible there is only one way to be saved or delivered and that is by Christ Jesus. All of mankind needs salvation. Since the fall of man the Bible declares that no one is righteous and all have sinned, "Surely there is not a righteous man on earth who does good and never sins" (Ecclesiastes 7:20 ESV); "for all have sinned and fall short of the glory of God," (Romans 2:23 ESV); "If we say we have no sin, we deceive ourselves, and the truth is not in us" (1 John 1:8 ESV). As we read in the following scriptures God alone, can remove and deliver us from penalty of sin, "who has saved us and called *us* with a holy calling, not according to our works, but according to His own purpose and grace which was given to us in Christ Jesus before time began" (2 Timothy 1:9 ESV); "not by works of righteousness which we have done, but according to His mercy He saved us, through the washing of regeneration and renewing of the Holy Spirit" (Titus 3:5).

How to Obtain Salvation:

How can you be saved and delivered from sin? The Bible says that we are saved by grace through our faith in Christ Jesus, "For by grace you have been saved through faith. And this is not your own doing; it is the gift of God" (Ephesians 2:8 ESV). This is how we obtain salvation, not even by our works. No amount of good deeds will get you into heaven. Isaiah said, "I will expose your righteousness and your works, and they will not benefit you" (Isaiah 57:12 ESV). It is only by Jesus and Him alone that salvation is obtained. Three things you must do to obtain salvation. First, you must hear the good news of Christ Jesus, His crucifixion, His death and burial, and His resurrection, "In him you also, when you heard the word of truth, the gospel of your salvation, and believed in him, were sealed with the promised Holy Spirit" (Ephesians 1:13 ESV). Second, you must believe and fully put your trust in Jesus as your Lord and Savior (Romans 10:10), and not be ashamed what He did for you by forgiving you from you transgressions, "For I am not ashamed of the gospel, for it is the power of God for salvation to everyone who believes, to the Jew first and also to the Greek" (Romans 1:16 ESV). Lastly, all of this involves you repenting, changing your mind, changing the direction you are headed, and going in the direction that God wants to you go; a new pathway to Christ. This pathway will deliver you from a pathway of death and destruction. Paul said to "Repent therefore, and turn back, that your sins may be blotted out" (Acts 3:19 ESV). Why? Because, "For everyone who calls on the name of the Lord will be saved" (Acts 10:13 ESV), that's why.

What is the Plan of Salvation?

We just learned about the three things you must do to obtain salvation, now let's talk about the plan of salvation and what that entails. The plan of salvation consists of three basic things, the *why*, the *who* and the *how*. The most important thing to remember is this not humanity's plan, but it is in fact, God's plan. The plan of man might consist of observing all types of religious rituals and obeying certain doctrinal beliefs and achieving some types of spiritual enlightenment, but that's not God's plan of salvation. None of these things can help you in receiving salvation God's way.

The Why: (Ecclesiastes 7:20 ESV; Romans 3:23; 1 John 1:8)

The very first thing we need to know and understand about salvation is why we need it. Why do we need to be saved? Saved from what? Here's a question I have been asked over the years and if you are a new believer you can rest assured that someone you know will ask you this same question, "what did you get saved from?" and this is your perfect opportunity to witness to them how you accepted Christ as your Lord and Savior. He rescued you from the flames of hell to one day live in heaven with Him. This is one great reason why we need to be saved. Sin, as we learned in the section "Sin", is a rebellion against God. Sin is harmful to one's health. It is harmful to others, it can damage relationships, and most important of all, it dishonors God.

The Bible is very clear when it says that God cannot allow sin to go unpunished, being He's a holy and just God. And the punishment for sin is death, "For the wages of sin is death, but the free gift of God is eternal life in Christ Jesus our Lord" (Romans 6:23 ESV). And this death and punishment is eternal and a separation from God Himself. The "why" is simple, we need salvation because we are sinners.

> "Then I saw a great white throne and him who was
> seated on it. From his presence earth and sky fled

away, and no place was found for them. 12 And I saw the dead, great and small, standing before the throne, and books were opened. Then another book was opened, which is the book of life. And the dead were judged by what was written in the books, according to what they had done. 13 And the sea gave up the dead who were in it, Death and Hades gave up the dead who were in them, and they were judged, each one of them, according to what they had done. 14 Then Death and Hades were thrown into the lake of fire. This is the second death, the lake of fire. 15 And if anyone's name was not found written in the book of life, he was thrown into the lake of fire" (Revelation 20:11-15 ESV).

The Who: (Matthew 16:15-16; John 1:1, 14)

The "who" referenced here is not the English rock band that started up in 1964. Depending on how old you are, you may not have a clue of who it is I am referring to. But the "who" I am talking about is none other than Jesus, the Christ Himself. He is the "who" from which we will receive the salvation we need. We are not capable of saving ourselves because of our sins and the consequences that come them. God became a human being and (here is the mind blowing mystery of this), He accomplished this through the Person of His Son Jesus Christ, "In the beginning was the Word, and the Word was with God, and the Word was God..." 14 "And the Word became flesh and dwelt among us, and we have seen his glory, glory as of the only Son from the Father, full of grace and truth" (John 1:1, 14 ESV).

Jesus was sinless, He lived a very sinless life offering Himself as a perfect sacrificial lamb on our behalf (2 Corinthians 5:21 ESV; Hebrews 4:15; 1 John 3:5; 1 Corinthians 15:3; Colossians 1:22; Hebrews 10:10). Jesus' death, was of infinite and eternal value; why? Because He was God, He died on the cross, and paid a debt we could not pay for the sins of the whole world, "He is the propitiation for our sins, and not for ours only but also for the sins of the whole world" (1 John 2:2 ESV). Salvation is available today because of Jesus' resurrection from the dead; it demonstrated that His sacrificial love was indeed enough for salvation.

The How: (Acts 16:31 ESV)

When you have heard the good news, and your heart has been convicted, you have a real emptiness to be filled. Your heart, your mind, and your soul want to know, "How do I receive salvation? What must I do to be saved?". This same question was asked of Paul and his response was, "Believe in the Lord Jesus, and you will be saved, you and your household" (Acts 16:31). This is the greatest "how" in receiving salvation. You must believe in Jesus Christ to Lord and Savior of all, and you will be saved. There is no magic formula, there are no motivational steps to salvation. Today, people want steps for this, and they want steps for that. There are steps on all types of "how to": how to lose weight, how to be more successful, how to get rich, how to find the right person. All these steps may be fine and dandy in the world of obtaining material goods and motivating people who need mental encouragement, but when it comes to salvation, there is only one true way (step), and that is through Jesus Christ.

The mistake many of us make in church leadership is trying to teach a step-by-step process of salvation. The Roman Catholic Church has the seven sacraments. Many different Christian denominations add public confession, turning from sin, baptism, speaking in tongues, and the list goes on as steps to salvation. In Islamic faith there are Five Pillars. Which, if they obey, grant salvation. It is also believed (by some, not all) that if they martyr themselves, 72 virgins are promised to them in paradise. The Bible is clear in pointing out and presenting only one step to salvation. What must you do to be saved? Do you know the step to take? (<u>Acts 16:31 ESV</u>; <u>Romans 10:9-10</u>). Listed are the Five Pillars of Islam and what they believe will grant salvation if obeyed (I am not promoting these beliefs).

Five Pillars of Islam:

1. **Shahada**: This is the Islamic proclamation that "There is no true God except Allah, and Muhammad is the Messenger of Allah."

2. **Prayer (Salat)**: Confessions of sins. Names of the prayers are Fajr, Dhuhr, Asr, Maghrib, Isha.

3. **Fasting (Saum)**: For the entire month of Ramadan there is no drinking, eating, or sexual relations during the daylight hours.

4. **Alms-giving of charity (Zakat)**: In order to move oneself towards more holiness and submission to Allah. You must give to the poor. It is considered a form of worship to God.

5. **Pilgrimage (Hajj)**: Muslims must make the pilgrimage the first half of the last month of the lunar year to Mecca.

When you truly trust what Jesus has done for us on the cross, and in no other works or steps, then that's when righteousness is given to you. Here is the trade-off; you give your sin to Him, He takes your sin, and He gives you righteousness. Trust in Jesus, believe in Him, obtain salvation, and you will never face the judgement of God, "My sheep hear My voice, and I know them, and they follow Me; 28 and I give eternal life to them, and they will never perish; and no one will snatch them out of My hand" (John 10:27-28 NIV). There are two things that distinguish the faith of Christianity from all other religions in the world. One, it's not a religion, it's a relationship with Christ. and two, there are no steps in which you must follow in order to receive salvation. The faith of a Christian recognizes that the steps have already been completed and simply said, it just calls on the repentant heart, by faith, to receive Him.

Salvation: Quiz

1. What is the definition of salvation?

2. Who is the only one that can save and deliver you from sin?

3. What two things must you do to obtain salvation?

    a.

    b.

4. The plan of salvation consists of three things, what are they?

    a.

    b.

    c.

5. What are the Five Pillars of Islam?

    a.   d.

    b.   e.

    c.

6. Two things that distinguish Christian faith from other religions are:

    a.

    b.

7. God requires five steps to be granted salvation (True or False).

8. God must punish the sinner (True or False).

9. Salvation is a gift you must work for (True or False).

10. Salvation is found in only one way, how?

Notes to Self:

Baptism

Peter replied, "Repent and be baptized, every one of you, in the name of Jesus Christ for the forgiveness of your sins. And you will receive the gift of the Holy Spirit.
(Acts 2:38 NIV)

To baptize to *immerse* in water, but first and foremost, let's address this one fact right out the gate; baptism is an outward, not an inward, proclamation of the conversion that takes place on the inside. The reason we need to understand this is because there has been more controversial rhetoric in Acts 2:38 regarding whether or not baptism is required for salvation. As we just learned, the one requirement for salvation is Jesus Christ, not baptism. There are many that teach using this verse, "Then Peter said to them, 'Repent, and let every one of you be baptized in the name of Jesus Christ for the remission of sins; and you shall receive the gift of the Holy Spirit'", that in order to be saved, one must be baptized. This verse and other verses used to teach salvation, do not in fact teach baptismal regeneration (that baptism is necessary for salvation, or that baptism saves).

Don't be fooled by this baptismal regeneration doctrine. It is important to know that with all the doctrines in our society, rarely are they generated from a single verse. In order to fully understand what God's word means in relation to a specific topic, we need to look and examine all of God's word, not just one verse that fits a present-day movement. Without going too deep in this (because it would have to be examined in a theology course to really do this justice) there are three exceptional ways to examine the word of God.

1. Examine its covenant context.

2. Examine its arrangement, grammar and structure.

3. Examine its dealings with forgiveness of sins.

God's word commanded for all people to repent of their sins. John the Baptist preached this day and night in the back deserts of Judaea (Matthew 3 NKJV). John preached repentance and baptized as many as would be baptized. He told the people that he indeed baptized them with water unto repentance (Matthew 3:11), but there was one coming that would baptize them with the Holy Ghost and with fire, which came to past on the day of Pentecost (Acts 2:3 NKJV).

Taking the message of John to heart, the people would believe and repent; thus, the new Christian would then be baptized. This is the outward identification of becoming a new believer (new convert, new creation), who has already repented. Acts 2:38 NKJV is not demonstrating that baptism is essential for one to receive salvation. It is the one thing we receive in order to totally identify ourselves publicly, with Christ. It is the inward manifestation, of the work that God has completed within us.

Even if you never attend a Bible college (although and I pray that you would), consider taking a course or two in religious studies (theology). It would be a great experience to learn about all types of religious studies as well as accounting and economics. I tend to believe that well rounded study brings a good balance into your life, both spiritually and naturally. But even if you take biblical courses, you will never find an entry in the Bible where it states that we are justified by grace and baptism. Nowhere will you find that we are saved by faith and baptism. But you will find that the Bible says we are saved by grace through faith, "For it is by grace you have been saved, through faith and this is not from yourselves, it is the gift of God" (Ephesians 2:8 NIV).

As you will learn in your biblical studies, baptism is totally excluded from the gospel messages. Look to what Paul said in 1 Corinthians when it came to this topic, "I thank God that I did not baptize any of you except Crispus and Gaius, 15 so no one can say that you were baptized in my name. 16 (Yes, I also baptized the household of

Stephanas; beyond that, I don't remember if I baptized anyone else.) 17 For Christ did not send me to baptize, but to preach the gospel—not with wisdom and eloquence, lest the cross of Christ be emptied of its power" (1 Corinthians 1:14-17 NIV).

Paul's message was clear, it was not about baptism. It was about the gospel; the resurrection of Christ. This is what he wrote in 1 Corinthians 15:1-4, "Now, brothers and sisters, I want to remind you of the gospel I preached to you, which you received and on which you have taken your stand. 2 By this gospel you are saved, if you hold firmly to the word, I preached to you. Otherwise, you have believed in vain. 3 For what I received I passed on to you as of first importance: that Christ died for our sins according to the Scriptures, that he was buried, that he was raised on the third day according to the Scriptures." As you can see, nowhere did Paul include, in the definition of the gospel, *baptism*. Baptism, it is not what saves us. Baptism is not part of salvation and baptism is not necessary for salvation. Baptism is what someone does who is already saved.

Baptism: Quiz

1. What does baptism mean?

2. Explain what baptism is.

3. How did John baptize?

4. How did Jesus baptize?

5. Does one have to be baptized in order to receive

salvation? _____ Why or why not?

6. This was excluded totally out of the gospel message:

_____.

7. What was Paul's message about?

8. What was Paul's message not about?

9. Baptism is what someone does who is already saved

(True or False).

10. Have you been baptized?

Notes to Self:

Pathway to Christ

Jesus said to him, "I am the way, and the truth, and the life. No one comes to the Father except through me"
(John 14:6 ESV)

Before Christ, what was the pathway to salvation? This may be a very confusing question for many, but have you ever thought about how people were saved in the Old Testament era? We know, by reading in the New Testament, that salvation comes by grace, and through faith, in Christ Jesus. And we also become the children of God (John 1:12 ESV; Ephesians 2:8-9).

There are many pathways in life as you may know. And the pathway you take in life can either take you to success or failure. How do you really determine which pathway you should take? As a child, your parents try to guide you, or dictate, the path you should take. Like most children you may not listen, or you may choose to take their route, but it's not your desire or dream. And your path should be one thing; of your own choosing (as long as it is not bringing harm to anyone). If you are truly happy and your path brings you joy, follow your heart and live your dreams to the fullest. Don't allow anyone to hinder your course to happiness. You have one life. You don't get a do-over. So, choose your pathway wisely.

To live a life on purpose should bring such joy because you are not bound by the rules and regulations of man. You are living a life that God has designed and created for you. In the book of Jeremiah, the prophet writes, "'For I know the plans I have for you' declares the LORD, 'plans to prosper you and not to harm you, plans to give you hope and a future'" (Jeremiah 29:11 NKJV). Sometimes we want to hear that God is going to prosper us and make us rich. We want to hear that He is going to move us from where we are to where we desire; in a big home, awesome job, great car, etc. But what about what God really meant in his verse? What about the preceding verses that tell a different story? A story that tell us to stay right where we are until those that are cursing and doing us wrong, are blessed and then we will be blessed? Oh no! That is not in "our plans", that can't be what God is saying!

In fact, that is what happened to the Israelites. Therefore, it is so important to examine the true context of what we read in the word of God. Things become a lot clearer. It is not to say that we will not be blessed, but it is to say that within our blessings there are some hard lessons to be learned. We just read, *plans to prosper you and not to harm you, plans to give you hope and a future.* And there really isn't anything wrong with that, per se. We just don't want to hear that we will have to suffer a little in order to receive that blessing. I know I don't. I tend to believe that I have suffered enough in life already, and I am ready for the blessings that God has promised me. Why should I have to suffer anymore? That's not fair. Have you thought this too? *I'm tired of people holding me back and stealing what rightfully belongs to me.* But the one thing I have learned thus far in life is *life is not fair.* That's right I admit that, it isn't, and I am shouting it as loud as I can, *LIFE IS NOT FAIR!* Can I get an Amen? Have I got a witness?!

Here is the other side of that unfairness that I have come to know very well and it has been somewhat of a mantra of mine down through the years, "No weapon that is formed against me will prosper" (Isaiah 54:17 KJV). This verse has comforted me much more than I can share. However, on example I will share, happened when I was going through my first divorce, yes, I did say first divorce (there have been a total of 3; a story for another time and another book). Even though life is not fair and very unpleasant at times, this verse is my reassurance that it will not always be that way. The verse did not say that I wouldn't have bad days, but it said it would not prosper. It did not say that I would not be disappointed, it said it would not prosper. It did not say that I would not have the money for rent or bills, but it said that it would not prosper. So, what does that tell you? It tells you that yes, problems, hardship, heartaches, and disappointments will happen, but the wonderful part about it is that it will not last always. And there is an end.

There are so many verses that are taken out of context and it is hurting the body of Christ. I am truly sorry to have to tell you this, especially if you are one that uses Jeremiah 29:11 for the sole purpose of reaping prosperity. Jeremiah 29:11 is not to be used as a security blanket. The true context of the verse is this; The Israelites had been exiled by Babylon as a punishment for their disobedience. The false prophet Hananiah boldly proclaimed the freedom of the Israelites from Babylon in two years. Jeremiah (true prophet of God) confronted Hananiah for lying to the people and falsely proclaiming their early release from bondage. Hananiah lied and Jeremiah called him out on it. This would be the paraphrased version of what Jeremiah said, *Hananiah, God has a plan indeed for the Israelites, and it is indeed a plan that will give His people hope and a prospering future.* However! Before he shared that promise, Jeremiah gave the Israelites God's directive, "And seek the peace of the city where I have caused you to be carried away captive and pray to the LORD for it; for in its peace you will have peace" (Jeremiah 29:7 NKJV). This was not what the Israelites wanted to hear. They did not want to be told that they had to stay right there and help prosper the nation that had enslaved them. But, in fact, God did command that. In verse 10, God says, "For thus says the LORD: After seventy years are completed at Babylon, I will visit you and perform My good word toward you and cause you to return to this place." Seriously! After seventy years? They wanted to hear that they were going home. They also wanted to hear that all their suffering had finally come to an end. But it was not so.

This meant that none of them (the current generation) would ever return home. They would never see their homeland again. What a devastating blow that was. But think for a moment, that was nothing more than what they deserved for being disobedient in the first place. It is a fact that God has a plan for us. And God will ultimately give us a glorious future. The one thing we must remember is, as we walk the pathway to Christ, enduring hardships, disappointments, and heartaches, that the best growth comes through persevering through the trials and not entirely escaping them. We will find unspeakable joy when we learn to persevere. Don't expect that you will not be punished for disobedience. It may not happen immediately, but rest assured, punishment is coming.

Here is the best way to uncover a false prophet, if they proclaim or declare something and it does not come to pass, or come true, then you know that they are a false prophet. There is no "oops" or, "I made a mistake, what I meant to say was". No, you lied, you false prophet! God clearly says, "when a prophet speaks in the name of the LORD, if the word does not come to pass or come true, that is a word that the LORD has not spoken; the prophet has spoken it presumptuously. You need not be afraid of him" (Deuteronomy 18:22 ESV). So be careful when someone whispers in your ear at a church revival that you are about to get a brand-new mansion or a boatload of money! Especially if they say you need to sow a thousand-dollar seed into their ministry. God does not need a thousand-dollar seed to bless you.

The pathway to Christ will not always be easy. There will be setbacks and heartaches. But while you are going through the tough times and you are in the midst of giving up, cling on to the words of Jeremiah 29:11. But be sure to cling on to it for the right reasons; not the false hope of thinking that God is going to take away the suffering just because of who you are, but, in the truth of His gospel, that He will give you hope in the midst of it all. The pathway can be good, it can be prosperous. The pathway to Christ, if you are obedient, holds a great future.

Pathway to Christ: Quiz

1. What does John 14:6 say?

2. What does Jeremiah 29:11 say?

3. Why were the Israelites punished by God?

4. What nation did God use to punish the Israelites?

5. Name the false prophet that Jeremiah confronted.

6. In how many years did the false prophet say the Israelites would be free?

7. How many years did God say the Israelites would be free?

8. Where is it found "when a prophet speaks in the name of the LORD, if the word does not come to pass or come true, that is a word that the LORD has not spoken; the prophet has spoken it presumptuously. You need not be afraid of him"?

9. Why isn't the pathway to Christ easy?

10. Have you decided your pathway to Christ?

Notes to Self:

Sinner's Prayer

that if you confess with your mouth the Lord Jesus and believe in your heart that God has raised Him from the dead, you will be saved. [10] For with the heart one believes unto righteousness, and with the mouth confession is made unto salvation
(Romans 10:9-10 NKJV)

How often have you heard about the sinner's prayer? I used to hear about the sinner's prayer every time we had a visiting preacher, evangelist, or prophet. After they got through preaching and ministering, they would offer up prayer for those who had not been saved. In other words, it was "alter call time" and after the alter call was made, there would be a few that were convicted by the word and felt compelled to come up for prayer or even give their life to Christ.

It was at this time the speaker would tell those who had come forward to repeat the "sinner's prayer". Let me explain my belief of the sinner's prayer; it is a prayer to God for those who understand that they are sinners and are in need of saving and a Savior. Just repeating a sinner's prayer will not accomplish anything on its own. A true heart felt sinner's prayer is one that only represents what the person knows, understands, and believes about their sin and their need for salvation.

What is the first aspect of a sinner's prayer? It is to understand that we are all sinners. The Bible says, "For all have sinned, and come short of the glory of God" (Romans 3:23 KJV). Paul said, "As it is written, there is none righteous, no, not one." The Bible is very clear that we are all sinners in need of mercy and forgiveness for the Father, "he saves us, not because of works done by us in righteousness, but according to his own mercy, by washing of regeneration and renewal of the Holy Spirit, 6 whom he poured out on us richly through Jesus Christ our Savior, 7 so that being justified by his grace we might become heirs according to the hope of eternal life" (Titus 3:5-7 ESV). We deserve eternal punishment because of our sin, "And these will go away into eternal punishment, but the righteous into eternal life" (Matthew 25:46 ESV). The sinner's prayer, instead of judgement, is a plea for grace. Instead of wrath, it is a request for mercy.

Knowing what God has done to remedy our lost and sinful condition is the second aspect of the sinner's prayer, "In the beginning was the Word, and the Word was with God, and the Word was God. 14 And the Word became flesh and dwelt among us, and we have seen his glory,

glory as of the only Son from the Father, full of grace and truth" (John 1:1, 14 ESV). In the Person of Jesus Christ, God took on flesh and became a human being. Jesus taught us the truth about God and lived a perfectly sinless and righteous life. He committed no sin, and no one could prove that he did, "Which one of you convicts me of sin? If I tell the truth, why do you not believe me?" (John 8:46). "For our sake he made him to be sin who knew no sin, so that in him we might become the righteousness of God" (2 Corinthians 5:21 ESV). Jesus rising from the dead was proof of His victory over sin, death and hell, "He disarmed the rulers and authorities and put them to open shame, by triumphing over them in him" (Colossians 2:15 ESV) (cf. 1 Corinthians 15 ESV).

We can now have our sins forgiven and be promised an eternal home in heaven, just by placing our faith in Christ Jesus because He died in our place and He rose from the dead for the redemption of our sins. It all starts with us confessing and then believing that we are saved, "because, if you confess with your mouth that Jesus is Lord and believe in your heart that God raised him from the dead, you will be saved. 10 For with the heart one believes and is justified, and with the mouth one confesses and is saved" (Romans 10:9-10 ESV). Paul declared, "For it is by grace you have been saved through faith. And this is not your own doing; it is the gift of God," (Ephesians 2:8 ESV).

Reciting the sinner's prayer is simply a way of declaring to God that you are, one, a sinner and two, that you confess and repent of your sins and three, believe that Jesus is the Christ, the Son of God who died on a cross, was buried and on the third day God raised Him up. And we too can be raised with Him.

In receiving salvation, there are no "magical words" it is only by your faith in Christ's death and resurrection that you can be saved. If you truly understand that you are a sinner in need of a Savior, and you are ready to say yes to Jesus today, then pray this prayer with me...

Dear Heavenly Father, I come to You admitting that I am a sinner in need of rescuing. Right now, I choose to turn away from my sin and I ask You to cleanse me of all unrighteousness. I believe that Your Son Christ Jesus died on the cross to take away my sins. I also believe that He rose again from the dead on the third day so that I might be forgiven of my sins and made righteous through faith in Him. I call upon the name of Christ Jesus and confess Him to be Lord and Savior of my life. Jesus, I say yes to You and I choose to follow You and ask You to fill me with the power of the Holy Spirit. I declare that right now I am a child of God. I am free from sin and full of the righteousness of God. I am saved in the name of Jesus. Amen.

If you prayed this prayer and said yes to receive Jesus Christ as your Lord and Savior, I welcome you to the family of God. From this moment on start learning more about how to live a life of faith by finding a good Holy Spirit filled, Bible taught church so that you can grow in your faith as you walk the pathway to Christ.

Notes to Self:

Saved

Then he brought them out and said, "Sirs, what must I do to be saved?
(Acts 16:30 ESV)

What can I do to be saved? What does it mean to be saved? These are two questions that we will attempt to address in this section of our workbook. "Being saved" is a phrase used a lot in the Christian faith. It is one of the most important question one can ask in life. It is a simple, yet, profound question that certainly needs to be answered. You can research different dictionaries to find an adequate answer to suit your desired curiosity. But in order to truly understand what it means to be saved; you will have to dig out your Bible.

What can I do to be saved?

What is the process of being saved? Is there a secret code or hand shake? Are there certain acts one must do to be saved? The one thing that the Bible talks about is where we will spend eternity after our life is over in this world. And being saved has a great deal to do with where we will spend eternity. Is there any other issue more important than where our eternal destiny will be? Nope! What is abundantly clear is that the Bible talks about how a person can be saved.

While the apostle Paul and Silas were in jail in Philippi, there was a Jailer that asked them the very question many are asking today, "Sirs, what must I do to be saved?" (Acts 16:30 ESV). Their response was simple and instant, "Believe in the Lord Jesus, and you will be saved" (Acts 16:31). Wait, that's it? You mean to tell me that we don't have to join a secret society? Nope! The Bible says that we are all infected with sin because of Adam and as a result of his sin we are all sinful, "for all have sinned and fall short of the glory of God" (Romans 3:23 ESV). In fact, we are all born in sin, "Behold, I was brought forth in iniquity, and in sin did my mother conceive me" (Psalms 51:5 ESV). My father would say that babies are beautiful bundles of sin. There is something that we do not have to teach children, and that is to lie. Ask them about the missing cookies and see what they say. "Did you eat those cookies?" They will look you right in the face and say, "No." You may not believe this but we all personally choose to sin. The Bible says, "Surely there is not a righteous man on earth who does good and never sins" (Ecclesiastes 7:20 ESV) and 1 John 1:8 says, "If we say we have no sin, we deceive ourselves, and the truth is not in us".

What makes us unsaved? That answer is sin. Sin is unrighteousness. And it separates us from God. The punishment for sin is eternal damnation and destruction. The Bible says that "the wages of sin is death" (Romans 6:23 ESV). What are wages? They are payments in return for work being done. So, if you commit sin, it is the same as working for evil and the payment for that sin is death. It's not a price I want to pay. Nor is it a payment I want to receive.

What does it mean, to be saved?

It is no secret that we all deserve the punishment for sin. It's the consequence for our physical sinful nature. Therefore, to be saved means being rescued from the eternal punishment of hell fire for sin, right along with Satan himself. The Bible says, "But the cowardly, unbelieving, abominable, murderers, sexually immoral, sorcerers, idolaters, and all liars shall have their part in the lake which burns with fire and brimstone, which is the second death" (Revelation 21:8 ESV). This is called the second death simply because it will follow the first death, which is the physical death of life. To be rescued from this type of death should be everyone's goal in life. Sadly, it is not. To get a real and most graphic portrayal of hell, you will need to read Revelation 14:9-11 NKJV.

God truly wants to save everyone. But He will not force His love or will upon anyone. To prove His love for mankind, He gave His only Son, Jesus Christ, to die and to sacrifice His life for us. Because of His death, burial, and resurrection, our sins are forgiven the moment we believe, confess and repent of our sin. We are then baptized into Jesus. God promises us that once we do this, we will receive "the gift of eternal life" (Romans 6:23 NKJV). This is how John puts it, "And this is the testimony: that God has given us eternal life, and this life is in His Son. 12 He who has the Son has life; he who does not have the Son of God does not have life" (1 John 5:11-12 NKJV). Can it be any simpler? I think not. You can have eternal life through Christ Jesus. It's a gift. This is what it means to be saved. We are saved (rescued) from eternal separation from God into outer darkness filled with pain and misery. Tormented in the flames of an unquenchable fire. You don't have to experience this punishment, no one does. It is a choice that we choose of our own free will. The Bible is filled with thousands of promises. One of the promises God makes and it is the very one I do not want to come to pass. Because we are guilty of sin, He promises eternal damnation in Hell. Listen, God is a God of mercy, but sin will be punished.

What do I need to do to be saved?

Finally, we can get to the most important part of our lesson and that is, *what you need to do to be saved*. Okay, here is what you need to do, and this is something that anyone can do, if they really want to be saved. It does not get any easier than this... God has already done the work for you, "For God so loved the world, that He gave His only begotten (Greek translation *monogenes*: "One and Only", "Only") Son, that whoever believes in Him should not perish but have everlasting life" (John 3:16 NKJV).

What you can do... (Romans 10:9-10)

Confess with your mouth the Lord Jesus (v.9)

Believe in your heart that God raised Him from the dead (v.10)

You will be saved.

It is with the heart that one believes unto righteousness. And it is with the mouth that confession is made unto salvation. That is all you need to do to be saved. This is the true Pathway to Christ.

Saved: Quiz

1. What does it mean to be saved?

2. What are the wages (payment) for sin?

3. Are you a sinner?

4. Do you believe that Jesus is the Son of God?

5. Do you believe that Jesus was crucified?

6. Do you believe that Jesus died?

7. Do you believe that God raised Jesus from the dead on the third day?

8. Are you ready to confess and repent of your sins?

9. Would you like to accept Jesus into your heart?

10. Are you ready to receive Christ as your Lord and Savior?

Pray this prayer: "Dear Heavenly Father, I come to You admitting that I am a sinner in need of rescuing. Right now, I choose to turn away from my sin and I ask You to cleanse me of all unrighteousness. I believe that Your Son Christ Jesus died on the cross to take away my sins. I also believe that He rose again from the dead on the third day so that I might be forgiven of my sins and made righteous through faith in Him. I call upon the name of Christ Jesus and confess Him to my Lord and Savior of my life. Jesus, I say yes to You and I choose to follow You and ask You to fill me with the power of the Holy Spirit. I declare that right now I am a child of God. I am free from sin and full of the righteousness of God. I am saved in the name of Jesus. Amen". If you prayed this prayer and said yes to receive Jesus Christ as your Lord and Savior, I welcome you to the family of God. From this moment on start learning more on how to live a life of faith by finding a good Holy Spirit filled, Bible taught church so that you can grow in your faith as you walk the pathway to Christ. I would love to hear from you.

Write to me, share your story of faith and let me know that you said yes to Jesus today. You can email me at lifeswordministry@gmail.com.

Notes to Self:

Scriptural References

abominations, 61 occurrences:
Lev. 18:26-27 (2 times), Lev. 18:29, Deut. 18:9, Deut. 18:12, Deut. 20:18, Deut. 32:16, 1 Ki. 14:24, 2 Ki. 16:3, 2 Ki. 21:2, 2 Ki. 21:11, 2 Chr. 28:3, 2 Chr. 33:2, 2 Chr. 34:33, 2 Chr. 36:8, 2 Chr. 36:14, Ezr. 9:1, Ezr. 9:11, Ezr. 9:14, Prov. 26:25, Jer. 7:10, Jer. 44:22, Ez. 5:9, Ez. 5:11, Ez. 6:9, Ez. 6:11, Ez. 7:3-4 (2x), Ez. 7:8-9 (2x), Ez. 7:20, Ez. 8:6 (2x), Ez. 8:9, Ez. 8:13, Ez. 8:15, Ez. 8:17, Ez. 9:4, Ez. 11:18, Ez. 11:21, Ez. 12:16, Ez. 14:6, Ez. 16:2, Ez. 16:22, Ez. 16:36, Ez. 16:43, Ez. 16:47, Ez. 16:51 (2x), Ez. 16:58, Ez. 18:13, Ez. 18:24, Ez. 20:4, Ez. 22:2, Ez. 23:36, Ez. 33:29, Ez. 36:31, Ez. 43:8, Ez. 44:6-7 (2x), Ez. 44:13

Abomination, 52 occurrences:
Gen. 43:32, Gen. 46:34, Exo. 8:26 (2 times), Lev. 18:22, Lev. 20:13, Deut. 7:25-26 (2x), Deut. 12:31, Deut. 13:14, Deut. 17:1, Deut. 17:4, Deut. 18:12, Deut. 22:5, Deut. 23:18, Deut. 24:4, Deut. 25:16, Deut. 27:15, 2 Ki. 23:13, Psa. 88:8, Prob. 3:32, Prob. 6:16, Prob. 8:7, Prob. 11:1, Prob. 11:20, Prob. 12:22, Prob. 13:19, Prob. 15:8-9 (2x), Prob. 15:26, Prob. 16:5, Prob. 16:12, Prob. 17:15, Prob. 20:10, Prob. 20:23, Prob. 21:27, Prob. 28:9 (2x), Prob. 29:27 (2x), Isa. 1:13, Isa. 41:24, Isa. 44:19, Jer. 2:7, Jer. 6:15, Jer. 8:12, Jer. 32:35, Ez. 16:50, Ez. 18:12, Ez. 22:11, Ez. 33:26, Mal. 2:11

Abominable, 4 occurrences:
Lev. 18:30, Deut. 14:3, Jer. 16:18, Jer. 44:4

N.T. References: Matt. 24:15, Lk. 16:14-15 (2 times), Rev. 21:27, Rev. 17:4-5 (2x)
Faith and Wisdom:

Hebrews 11; John 10:10; Romans 12:2; 1 Corinthians 2:5-
10, 14; 13:12; James 1:2-4

Heaven:
Deuteronomy 26:15; 1 King 8:30; 2 Chronicles 30:27; Job
22:12; Psalms 73:25; 123:1; Isaiah 66:1 Luke 11:2; Acts
7:49

Heavens:
Genesis 1:1; 1 Chronicles 16:26 Psalms 102:25; Proverbs
8:27; Isaiah 40:22; 42:5; 45:12; Jeremiah 32:17

Hell:
Matthew 25:41
Luke 16:24

New Creation:
2 Corinthians 5:17

Partiality/Favoritism:
James 2:1-13

Paul's Conversion:
Acts 9

Salvation:
Romans 10:9-10; Philippians 3:4-11

Summary of Paul's Sufferings:
2 Corinthians 11:21-33

The Cleansing of the Temple:
John 2:13-22

The Crucifixion of Christ:

Matthew 27

The Day of Pentecost:
Acts 2

The Day of Pentecost:
Act 2

The First Sin:
Genesis 3

The Five "I Wills of Satan":
Isaiah 14:13-14

The Jailers Conversion:
Act 16:25-34

The Stoning of Stephen:
Acts 6 and 7

The Trinity (Godhead):
Genesis 1:1, 26; 3:22; 11:7; Isaiah 6:8, 48:16, 61:1;
Matthew 3:16-17, 28:19; 2 Corinthians 13:14

The Way:
John 14:6

Trials and Joy:
1 Peter 1:6-9

Recommended Resources

Destruction and Rebuilding of the Temple:
Retrieved from
https://www.bibleodyssey.org/en/places/related-articles/destruction-and-reconstruction-of-the-temple.aspx

Jehovah Witness on Tongues:
Retrieved from https://www.jw.org/en/bible-teachings/questions/speaking-in-tongues/

Ekklesia:
Thayer and Smith. (1999). "Greek Lexicon entry for Ekklesia". "The NAS New Testament Greek Lexicon".

Examination of Acts 2:38:
Retrieved from https://carm.org/baptism-and-acts-238

Fairchild, M. (2018) "Top Books About Heaven"
ThoughtCo. Retrieved from
https://www.thoughtco.com/top-books-about-heaven-700313

Five Pillars of Islam:
Retrieved from
http://www.islam101.com/dawah/pillars.html

Four Views on Hell:
Retrieved from https://www.christianbook.com/four-views-on-hell/john-walvoord/9780310212683/pd/21268?event=AFF&p=1011693&

Heaven:
heaven. (n.d.) *American Heritage® Dictionary of the English Language, Fifth Edition.* (2011). Retrieved April 5, 2019 from https://www.thefreedictionary.com/heaven

Pew Research Center: Most Americans Believe in Heaven...
Retrieved from https://www.pewforum.org/2015/11/03/u-s-public-becoming-less-religious/

Roman Catholic Church:
Retrieved from The Gospel According to Rome: Comparing Catholic Tradition and The Word of God by James McCarthy)

Salvation:
The New Dictionary of Cultural Literacy, Third Edition.
Retrieved from
https://www.dictionary.com/browse/salvation

Smith, W. (1901) Sanhedrin:
Retrieved from
https://www.biblestudytools.com/dictionaries/smiths-bible-dictionary/sanhedrin.html

The Holy Spirit:
Retrieved from The Holy Spirit by Charles Ryrie

72 Virgins:
Retrieved from http://www.aviperry.org/political-blogs/where-did-the-notion-of-72-virgins-in-islamic-paradise-come-from

About the Author

 **Pastor Malachi** was born and raised in San Diego, California. For 10 years, Malachi modeled and acted on several local theatrical shows as well as many movies and TV commercials.

His other career endeavors include working as an employee for the City of San Diego. He was forced into early retirement after a terrible on -the-job vehicle accident which launched him into his entrepreneurship journey.

Pastor Malachi received his bachelor's and master's degree in Christian Studies with an Emphasis in Leadership from Grand Canyon University, AZ. His ministry endeavors include becoming a licensed and ordained minister in 1984; Youth Leader from 1998-2008 then Youth Pastor from 2008-2014 and has been the Co-Pastor at Good Samaritan Church of San Diego alongside his brother, who is currently the Assistant Pastor to their father and mother, Senior Pastor Bishop Henry Mitchell, Jr. and Lady Lola Mitchell.

God placed a vision in Malachi after he retired from the City of San Diego, where he also became the founder of "The Spoken Word Ministries". Recently, God moved upon him to rename it "Life's WORD Ministry" in 2017.

In 2011 Pastor Malachi became Facebook friends via LegalShield (formerly known as Pre-Paid Legal), with Christine. After finally meeting in person August of 2016, at a bonfire in San Diego (arranged by Pastor Malachi), Pastor Malachi and Christine realized that God had a greater divine purpose for their lives. In October of 2017 they were united as husband and wife. Between the two of them they have 7 children and 3 grandchildren.

Together, their mission is to reach, teach, empower, encourage, uplift and motivate people of all ages. They want to help in the healing process of battered mothers and children and reconnect children with their absentee fathers. It is their endeavor to correct many of the societal mistakes that have caused an increase in homeless men, women and children and to help rebuild family structure. One of their many goals is to help those that are less fortunate, to regain a sense of appreciation for life again through many of their self-awareness workshops. The core value of their ministry is founded on Biblical principal; reclaiming, rebuilding, and restoring peoples trust and helping them to **Live** in **Hope,** and **Change**.

Writing has always been a passion of Malachi's, but he never really pursued it seriously until now. Training and teaching are a true calling in his life and one that he loves to do, so writing a Christian workbook is a dream come true.

Quiz Answers

In the Beginning:
1. Paul.
2. "If you confess with your mouth that Jesus is Lord…you will be saved".
3. Grace, Gift, Faith, Speak.
4. Salvation or They are saved.
5. That if you confess with your mouth the Lord Jesus and believe in your heart that God had raised Him from the dead, you will be saved. 10. For with the heart one believes unto righteousness, and with the mouth confession is made unto salvation.
6. Open answer
7. Paul.
8. Tarsus.
9. Damascus. To round up Christians to kill.
10. Events in Paul's life:
   *The witnessing of Stephen's stoning
   *Received three years of personal teaching Jesus, while living in Arabia
   *Resurrected at least one person from the dead
   *Carried out at least five evangelistic journeys
   *Visited more than 50 cities
   *Five times received thirty-nine stripes
   *Beaten three times with rods
   *Stoned once
   *Shipwrecked three times
   *Was Robbed

*Bitten by a snake

*Left out in the cold naked, thirsty and hungry

*Let down a wall in a basket to escape the governor under Aretas the king

*Preached the gospel to Emperor Caesar and his entire household

*Wrote no less than fourteen books (epistles/letters) of the Bible (no other author can say that)

*Trained & instructed other evangelists and preachers of the gospel (John Mark and Timothy)

*Endured more than five years in prison

In the Middle:

1. a. The Joy the World Gives, Is Not the Same Joy That God Gives.

    b. God's Joy Cannot Be Taken Away.

    c. You Have to Grab onto God's Joy.

2. No. At times they may seem to be amplified.

3. He encouraged and instruct them to have faith in their trials; that their faith could develop perseverance.

4. Five things Peter was known for:

    a. Being one of Jesus' disciples.

    b. The one called the "Rock".

    c. Walking on water.

    d. Cutting off a man's ear in the Garden of Gethsemane.

    e. Denying Christ three times.

5. Be strong and courageous. Do not be afraid or terrified because of them, for the LORD your God goes with you; he will never leave you nor forsake you.

6. True joy comes in your walk of faith.

7. Joy, Lord, Strength.

8. Joy.

9. Persecuted.

10. Grab onto it.

What Faith…Now Faith

1. What is one of the most important elements in a person's life?

2. What are the two aspects of faith?

   a. Faith.

   b. You must believe.

3. Even the demons believe and shudder.

4. "For by *grace* you have been saved through faith. And this is not your own doing; it is the gift of God, not a result of works, as that no one may boast" (Ephesians 2:8-9 ESV).

5. It is the gift of God.

6. Faith.

7. Pure joy.

8. By drawing closer to God through praying and studying His Word.

9. Be anxious for nothing, but in everything by prayer and supplication, with thanksgiving, let your requests, be made known to God; and the peace of God, which surpasses all understanding, will guard your hearts and minds through Christ Jesus.

10. a. By confessing our sins (John 1:7 NKJV; 1 John 1:9 NKJV).

   b. By seeking Him (Ps. 27:8 NKJV; Isa. 55:6 NKJV).

   c. By Surrendering to Him (Gal. 3:3 NKJV; Col 2:6 NKJV; Rom. 12:1 NKJV).

New Creation:

1. Therefore, if anyone *is* in Christ, he *is* a new creation; old things have passed away; behold, all things have become new.
2. Open Answer.
3. Nature, Nailed, Cross, Jesus.
4. Lovers of sin. b. Natural pride. c. Passions. d. Bad habits. e. Unnatural affections.
f. Reliance of works.
5. Life. Dead.
6. 1 Corinthians 15:31
7. If you have been set free from sin, say so by testifying what God has done in your life.
8. True.
9. False.
10. Creation.

Be the Church:

1. Peter.
2. Act 2.
3. "an assembly" or better yet, "called-out, from the world for God".
4. False.
5. False.
6. False.
7. True.
8. 120
9. By sacrificially giving your all to and for Christ.
10. Open answer.

The Holy Spirit:

1. Spirit.
2. God the Father. God the Son. God the Holy Spirit.

3. Comforter/Counselor/Helper/Advocate/Intercessor/
Author/The Lord/Christ/Witness
4. The Book of the Holy Spirit.
5. By the Holy Spirit.
6. The Holy Spirit.
7. They were first cousins.
8. Elizabeth.
9. "Go ye therefore, and make disciples of all the nations,
baptizing them into the name of the Father, and of the Son
and of the Holy Spirit".
10. Open answer.

Tongues:
1. In the Book of Acts (Act 2:1-4 NIV)
2. Languages.
3. False.
4. False.
5. What are two reasons mentioned that the Holy Spirit was
given?
    a. to edify the Body of Christ.
    b. to glorify God.
6. "For by grace are ye saved through faith; and that not of
yourselves: *it is* the gift of God"
7. a. Private prayer language.
    b. Tongue that is interpreted.
    c. Tongue of missionary context.
8. What is the importance of speaking in tongues?
9. The believe that tongues have ceased.
10. Open answer.

Heaven:
1. Open answer.
2. God.

3. Genesis 1:1.

4. John 14:2

5. Through Jesus.

6. In Heaven.

7. It is the dwelling place of God. A place of fellowship and eternal joy.

8. Wherever God is.

9. 276 times.

10. To one day see God face to face in our new home, heaven.

Hell:

1. Hell.

2. Gehenna.

3. "a star that had fallen from the sky to earth".

4. Isaiah 14:13-14

    a. I will ascend into heaven.

    b. I will exalt my throne above the stars of God.

    c. I will sit also upon the mount of the congregation.

    d. I will ascend above the heights of the clouds.

    e. I will be like the Most High.

5. a. P – Position.

    b. R – Rule.

    c. I – Idolized.

    d. D – Dominion.

    e. E – Equality.

6. For Satan and those angels that rebelled against God.

7. Open answer.

8. For sinning. Turning their backs on God. Rejecting Him.

9. Salvation/Jesus Christ.

10. Being casted into the lake of fire.

Sin:

1. Sin is transgression against the laws of God.
2. Hamartiology.
3. Lucifer.
4. Deceiving.
5. Their spiritual eyes came open. They spiritually died.
6. They were kicked out the garden.
7. A snake.
8. a. Proud look.
   b. Lying tongue.
   c. Murder.
   d. Heart that devises wicked.
   e. Feet that are swift in running to evil.
   f. One who sows discord among brethren.
9. All who behave unrighteous.
10. [9] that if you confess with your mouth the Lord Jesus and believe in your heart that God has raised Him from the dead, you will be saved. [10] For with the heart one believes unto righteousness, and with the mouth confession is made unto salvation.

Salvation:

1. "Preservation or deliverance from harm, ruin, or loss".
2. Jesus.
3. a. First, you must hear the good news of Christ Jesus, His crucifixion, His death and burial, and His resurrection.
   b. Second, you must believe and fully put your trust in Jesus as your Lord and Savior (Romans 10:10), and not be ashamed what He did for you by forgiving you from you transgressions.
4. a. The Why.
   b. The Who.

c. The How.

5. What are the Five Pillars of Islam?

    a. Shahada d. Alms-giving of charity

    b. Prayer   e. Pilgrimage

    c. Fasting

6. Two things that distinguish Christian faith from other religions are:

    a. One, it's not a religion, it's a relationship with Christ.

    b. two, there are no steps in which you must follow in order to receive salvation.

7. False.

8. True.

9. False.

10. "For by grace you have been saved through faith. And this is not your own doing; it is the gift of God" (Ephesians 2:8 ESV).

Baptism:

1. To immerse in water.

2. baptism is an outward, not an inward, proclamation of the conversion that takes place on the inside.

3. John baptized with water unto repentance.

4. With the Holy Ghost and with fire.

5. No. Baptism, it is not what saves us. Baptism is not part of salvation and baptism is not necessary for salvation. Baptism is what someone does who is already saved.

6. Baptism.

7. The gospel; the resurrection of Christ.

8. Baptism.

9. True.

10. Open answer.

Pathway to Christ:

1. Jesus said to him, "I am the way, the truth, and the life. No one comes to the Father except through me"

2. For I know the plans I have for you,' says the Lord, 'plans for well-being and not for trouble, to give you a future and a hope.

3. The Israelites had been exiled as a punishment for their disobedience.

4. Babylon.

5. Hananiah.

6. Two years.

7. Seventy years.

8. Deuteronomy 18:22.

9. There will be setbacks and heartaches.

10. Open answer.

****

A Message to My Readers:

Pathway to Christ was created to be a simple workbook to learn simple fundamentals of walking a pathway of godliness and living a life by faith.

Thank you for your prayers, love, and support. If you would like to sow into this ministry you can do so by going to: PayPal.me/lifeswordministry

Website: www.lifeswordministry.org

Mailing Address: P.O. Box 96 | Wildomar | CA | 92595

Made in the USA
Middletown, DE
27 September 2020